Three Union Army Regiments

Three Union Army Regiments

of the American Civil War

The County Regiment
Dudley Landon Vaill

History of the Second Massachusetts
Regiment of Infantry
Daniel Oakey

Frontier Service During the Rebellion
George H. Pettis

LEONAUR

Three Union Army
Regiments
of the American Civil War
The County Regiment by Dudley Landon Vaill
History of the Second Massachusetts
Regiment of Infantry by Daniel Oakey
Frontier Service During the Rebellion by George H. Pettis

First published under the titles
The County Regiment,
History of the Second Massachusetts
Regiment of Infantry
and
Frontier Service During the Rebellion

Leonaur is an imprint of Oakpast Ltd

ISBN: 978-0-85706-108-9 (hardcover)
ISBN: 978-0-85706-107-2 (softcover)

http://www.leonaur.com

Contents

GOVERNOR BUCKINGHAM

The County Regiment

Dudley Landon Vaill

Contents

Prefatory

For those who dwell within its borders, or whose ancestral roots are bedded among its hills, the claims of Litchfield County to distinction are many and of many kinds. In these latter days it has become notable as the home of certain organizations of unique character and high purpose, which flourish under circumstances highly exceptional, and certainly no less highly appreciated.

It is as part of the work of one of these that there is commemorated in this volume an organization of an earlier day, one distinctively of the county, in no way unique in its time, but of the highest purpose—the regiment gathered here for the national defence in the Civil War.

The county's participation in that defence was by no means restricted to the raising of a single regiment. Quite as many, perhaps more, of its sons were enrolled in other commands as made up what was known originally as the Nineteenth Connecticut Volunteer Infantry; but in that body its organized effort as a county found expression, and it was proud to let the splendid record of that body stand as typical of its sacrifices for the preservation of the Union.

Though the history of that regiment's career has been written in full detail, the purpose of this slight repetition of the story needs no apology. There is sufficient justification in its intrinsic interest, to say nothing of a personal interest in its members, men who gave such proofs of their quality, and whose survivors are still our neighbours in probably every town in the county.

There is also something more than mere interest to be gained, in considering historical matters of such immensity as the Civil War, in giving the attention to some minute section of the whole, such as the account of individual experiences, or of the career of a particular regiment such as this; it is of great value as bringing an adequate realization of the actual bearing of the great events of that time upon the people of the time. The story of a body of Litchfield County men, such men as we see every day, drawn from such homes as we know all about us, is a potent help to understanding in what way and with what aspects these great historical movements bore upon the people of the country, for the experience of this group of towns and their sons furnished but one small instance of what was borne, infinitely magnified, throughout the nation.

It will readily appear that the subject might furnish material for a notable volume. In the present case nothing is possible save a brief sketch of the matter, made up chiefly, as will be seen, of citations from the published history of the regiment, and from such other sources of information as were easily accessible. Among the latter must be noted the records of the Regimental Association, to which access was had through the courtesy of its secretary, D. C. Kilbourn, Esq., of Litchfield, and his assistance, as well as that of H. W. Wessells, Esq., of Litchfield, to both of whom the securing of most of the illustrations used is due, is gratefully acknowledged.

The County Regiment

In spite of the labours of unnumbered chroniclers, it is not easy, if indeed it is possible, for us of this later generation to realize adequately the great patriotic uprising of the war times.

It began in the early days of 1861 with the assault on Fort Sumter, which, following a long and trying season of uncertainty, furnished the sudden shock that resolved the doubts of the wavering and changed the opinions of the incredulous. Immediately there swept over all the northern states a wave of intense national feeling, attended by scenes of patriotic and confident enthusiasm more noisy than far-sighted, and there was a resulting host of volunteers, who went forth for the service of ninety days with the largest hopes, and proportionate ignorance of the crisis which had come to the nation. Of these Connecticut furnished more than her allotted share, and Litchfield County a due proportion.

The climax of this excited period was supplied by the battle of Bull Run. There was surprise, and almost consternation, at the first news of this salutary event, but quickly following, a renewed rally of patriotic feeling, less excited but more determined, and with a clearer apprehension of the actual situation. The enlistment of volunteers for a longer term had been begun, and now went forward briskly for many months; regiment after regiment was enrolled, equipped, and sent southward, until, in the spring of 1862, the force of this movement began to spend itself.

The national arms had met with some important successes during the winter, and a feeling of confidence had arisen in the invincibility of the Grand Army of the Potomac, which had been gathering and organizing under General McClellan for what the impatient country was disposed to think an interminable time. A War Department order in April, 1862, putting a stop to recruiting for the armies, added to the confidence, since an easy inference could be drawn from it, and the North settled down to await with high hopes the results of McClellan's long expected advance.

Then came the campaign on the Peninsula. At first there was but meagre news and a multitude of conflicting rumours about its fierce battles and famous retreat, but in the end the realization of the failure of this mighty effort. To the country it was a disappointment literally stunning in its proportions; but now at length there was revealed the magnitude of the task confronting the nation, and again there sprang up the determination, grim and intense, to strain every nerve for the restoration of the Union.

The President's call for three hundred thousand men to serve "for three years or the war" was proclaimed to this state by Governor Buckingham on July 3rd (1862), and evidence was at once forthcoming that it was sternly heeded by the people. To fill Connecticut's quota under this call, it was proposed that regiments should be raised by counties. A convention was promptly called, which met in Litchfield on July 22nd; delegates from every town in the county were in attendance, representatives of all shades of political opinion and individual bias, but the conclusions of the meeting were unanimously reached. It was resolved that Litchfield County should furnish an entire regiment of volunteers, and that Leverett W. Wessells, at that time Sheriff, should be recommended as its commander.

Immediate steps were taken to render this determination effective; the Governor promptly accepted the recommendation as to the colonelcy, recruiting officers were designated to secure enlistments, bounties voted by the different towns as proposed by the county meeting, and the movement thoroughly organized. Although there was a clear appreciation of the present need, the dozen or more Connecticut regiments already in the field had drawn a large number of men from Litchfield County, and effort was necessary to gain the required enrolment.

There had been many opportunities already for all to volunteer who had any wish to do so, but the call now came to men who a few weeks before had hardly dreamed of the need of their serving; men not to be attracted by the excitement of a novel adventure, but who recognized soberly the duty that was presenting itself in this emergency, and men of a very different stamp from those drawn into the ranks in the later years of the war by enormous bounties.

It is reasonable to think that pride in the success of the county's effort was a factor in stimulating enlistments; announcement that a draft would be resorted to later was doubtless another. Just at this time, also, the return from a year's captivity in the South of the Rev. Hiram Eddy of Winsted, who had been made prisoner at Bull Run, furnished a powerful advocate to the cause; night after night he spoke in different towns, urging the call to service fervently and with effect.

It is to be noted that at the same time that this endeavour was being made to fill the ranks of a regiment for three years' service, recruiting was going on with almost equal vigour under the call for men to serve for nine months, and three full companies were contributed by Litchfield County to the Twenty-eighth Infantry, which bore a valiant part in the campaign against Port Hudson in the following summer. It is possible to gain some idea of how the great tides of war were felt throughout the whole land by imagining the stir and turmoil thus brought, in the summer of 1862, into this remote and peaceful quarter by the engrossing struggle.

In the last week in August, the necessary number of recruits having been secured, the different companies were brought together in Litchfield and marched to the hill overlooking the town which had been selected as the location of Camp Dutton, named in honour of Lieutenant Henry M. Dutton, who had fallen in battle at Cedar Mountain shortly before. Lieutenant Dutton, the son of Governor Henry Dutton, was a graduate of Yale in the class of 1857, and was practising law in Litchfield when he volunteered for service on the organization of the Fifth Connecticut Infantry.

The interest and pride of the county in its own regiment was naturally of the strongest; the family that had no son or brother or cousin in its ranks seemed almost the exception, and Camp Dutton became at once the goal of a ceaseless stream of visitors from far and near, somewhat to the prejudice of those principles of military order and discipline which had now to be acquired. The preparation and drill which employed the scant two weeks spent here were supervised by Lieutenant-Colonel Kellogg, fresh from McClellan's army in Virginia, and he was afterwards reported as delivering the opinion that if there were nine hundred men in the camp, there were certainly nine thousand women most of the time.

With all possible haste, preparations were made for an early departure, but there was opportunity for a formal mustering of the regiment in Litchfield, when a fine set of colours was presented by William Curtis Noyes, Esq., on behalf of his wife. A horse for the colonel was given also, by the Hon. Robbins Battell, saddle and equipments by Judge Origen S. Seymour, and a sword by the deputies who had served under Sheriff Wessells.

On September 15th (1862), the eight hundred and eighty-nine officers and men now mustered as the Nineteenth Connecticut Volunteer Infantry broke camp, made their first march to East Litchfield station, and started for the South, with the entire population for miles around gathered to witness, not as a holiday spectacle, but as a farewell, grave with significance, the departure of the county regiment.

"In order to raise it," says the regimental history, "Litchfield County had given up the flower of her youth, the hope and pride of hundreds of families, and they had by no means enlisted to fight for a superior class of men at home. There was no superior class at home. In moral qualities, in social worth, in every civil relation, they were the best that Connecticut had to give. More than fifty of the rank and file of the regiment subsequently found their way to commissions, and at least a hundred more proved themselves not a whit less competent or worthy to wear sash and sabre if it had been their fortune."

The regimental officers were: Colonel, Leverett W. Wessells, Litchfield; lieutenant-colonel, Elisha S. Kellogg, Derby; major, Nathaniel Smith, Woodbury; adjutant, Charles J. Deming, Litchfield; quartermaster, Bradley D. Lee, Barkhamsted; chaplain, Jonathan A. Wainwright, Torrington; surgeon, Henry Plumb, New Milford.

Colonel Wessells, a native of Litchfield, and a brother of General Henry W. Wessells of the regular army, had been prominent in public affairs before the war, and served for twelve years as Sheriff. Ill health interfered with his service with the regiment from the first, and finally compelled his resignation in September, 1863. Later he was appointed Provost Marshal for the Fourth District of Connecticut, and for many years after the war was active in civil affairs, being the candidate for State Treasurer on the Republican ticket in 1868, Quartermaster-General on Governor Andrews' staff, and member of the General Assembly. He died at Dover, Delaware, April 4, 1895.

Washington in September, 1862, while relatively secure from the easy capture which would have been possible in the summer of the previous year, was not in a situation of such safety as to preclude anxiety, for Pope had just been beaten at Bull Run and Lee's army was north of the Potomac in the first of its memorable invasions of the

Rev. Hiram Eddy

Presentation of colours, September 10th, 1862

loyal states. On the very day of his check at Antietam, September 17th, the Nineteenth Connecticut Volunteers reached the capital, and the next day moved into the hostile state of Virginia, bivouacking near Alexandria.

In this vicinity the regiment was destined to remain for many months, and to learn, as far as was possible without the grim teachings of actual experience, the business for which it was gathered. At first there was a constant expectation of orders to join the army in active operations; the county newspapers for many weeks noted regularly that the regiment was still near Alexandria, "but orders to march are hourly expected." It was good fortune, however, that none came, for not a little of the credit of its later service was due to the proficiency in discipline and soldierly qualities gained in the long months now spent in preparation.

The task of giving the necessary military education to the thousand odd men fresh from the ordinary routine of rural Connecticut life, fell upon the shoulders of Lieutenant-Colonel Kellogg, and by all the testimony available, most of all by the splendid proof they later gave, it is clear that it was entrusted to a master hand. Matters of organization and administration at first engrossed Colonel Wessells' attention; ill health soon supervened, and later he was given the command of a brigade. The regiment from its beginning was Kellogg's, and he received in due course the commission vacated by its first commander in September, 1863.

A thorough and well-tried soldier himself, he quickly gained the respect of his command by his complete competency, and its strong and admiring affection was not slow in following. There are men among us to this day for whom no superlatives are adequate to give expression to their feelings in regard to him. As the regimental history records of their career:

> ... there is not a scene, a day, nor a memory from Camp Dutton to Grapevine Point that can be wholly divested of Kellogg. Like the ancient Eastern king who suddenly died on the eve of an engagement, and whose remains were bolstered up in warlike attitude in his chariot, and followed by his enthusiastic soldiers to battle and to victory, so this mighty leader, although falling in the very first onset, yet went on through every succeeding march and fight, and won posthumous victories for the regiment which may be said to have been born of his loins.

> Battalion and company, officer and private, arms and quarters,

camp and drill, command and obedience, honour and duty, esprit and excellence, every moral and material belonging of the regiment, bore the impress of his genius. In the eyes of civilians, Colonel Kellogg was nothing but a horrid, strutting, shaggy monster. But request any one of the survivors of the Nineteenth Infantry or the Second Artillery to name the most perfect soldier he ever saw, and this will surely be the man.

Or ask him to conjure up the ideal soldier of his imagination, still the same figure, complete in feature, gesture, gauntlet, sabre, boot, spur, observant eye and commanding voice, will stalk with majestic port upon the mental vision. He seemed the superior of all superiors, and major-generals shrunk into pigmy corporals in comparison with him. In every faculty of body, mind, heart, and soul he was built after a large pattern. His virtues were large and his vices were not small.

As Lincoln said of Seward, he could swear magnificently. His nature was versatile, and full of contradictions; sometimes exhibiting the tenderest sensibilities and sometimes none at all. Now he would be in the hospital tent bending with streaming eyes over the victims of fever, and kissing the dying Corporal Webster, and an hour later would find him down at the guard house, prying open the jaws of a refractory soldier with a bayonet in order to insert a gag; or in anger drilling a battalion, for the fault of a single man, to the last point of endurance; or shamefully abusing the most honourable and faithful officers in the regiment. 'In rage, deaf as the sea, hasty as fire.'

But notwithstanding his frequent ill treatment of officers and soldiers, he had a hold on their affections such as no other commander ever had, or could have. The men who were cursing him one day for the almost intolerable rigors of his discipline, would in twenty-four hours be throwing up their caps for him, or subscribing to buy him a new horse, or petitioning the Governor not to let him be jumped. The man who sat on a sharp-backed wooden horse in front of the guard house, would sometimes watch the motions of the colonel on drill or parade, until he forgot the pain and disgrace of his punishment in admiration of the man who inflicted it.

It is not hard to understand the hold he gained, through a personality so striking and forceful, upon the men of his command; they were but boys for the most part, in point of fact, and open to the influence

CAMP. 19TH REGT CONN VOLS:
near Alexandria Va
Col L. W. Wessels Comd.

THE FIRST ENCAMPMENT IN VIRGINIA

of just such strength, and perhaps also just such weaknesses, as they saw in this splendidly virile and genuine, and very human character.

Colonel Kellogg was a Litchfield County man, a native of New Hartford, and at this time about thirty-eight years of age. His education was not of the schools, but gained from years of adventurous life as sailor, gold-hunter, and wanderer. Shortly before the war he had settled in his native state, but he responded to the call for the national defence among the very first, and before the organization of the Nineteenth had served as Major of the First Connecticut Artillery. He lies buried in Winsted.

For more than a year and a half the regiment was numbered among the defenders of the capital, removing after a few months from the immediate neighbourhood of Alexandria, and being stationed among the different forts and redoubts which formed the line of defence south of the Potomac.

Important as its service there was, and novel as it must have been to Litchfield County boys, it was not marked by incidents of any note, and furnished nothing to attract attention among the general and absorbing operations of the war. It was, still, of vast interest to the people of the home towns. The county newspapers had many letters to print in those days from the soldiers themselves, and from visitors from home, who in no inconsiderable numbers were journeying down to look in upon them constantly.

There were of course matters of various nature which gave rise to complaints of different degrees of seriousness; there was not unnaturally much sickness among the men in the early part of their service; there were political campaigns at home, in which the volunteers had and showed a strong interest; there was a regrettable quarrel among the officers in which Lieutenant-Colonel Kellogg was placed in an unfortunate light, and the termination of which gave the men an opportunity of showing their feeling for him. All these matters were well aired in type; meanwhile the regiment, doing well such duty as was laid upon it, grew in efficiency for hard and active service when it should be called for.

The possibility of a call to action at almost any minute was seen in April, 1863, when orders came that the regiment be held ready to march. Reinforcements were going forward to the Army of the Potomac, now under Hooker, in large numbers; but the Nineteenth was finally left in the Defences. Thus months were passed in the routine of drill and parade, guard mounting and target practice, varied by brief and rare furloughs, while the lightnings of the mighty conflict raging so near left them untouched.

"Yet," it is related, "a good many seemed to be in all sorts of affliction, and were constantly complaining because they could not go to the front. A year later, when the soldiers of the Nineteenth were staggering along the Pamunkey, with heavy loads and blistered feet, or throwing up breastworks with their coffee-pots all night under fire in front of Petersburg, they looked back to the Defences of Washington as to a lost Elysium."

It was in November, 1863, that the War Department orders were issued changing the Nineteenth Infantry to a regiment of heavy artillery, which Governor Buckingham denominated the Second Connecticut. Artillery drill had for some time been part of its work, and the general efficiency and good record of the regiment in all particulars was responsible for the change, which was a welcome one, as the artillery was considered a very desirable branch of the service, and the increase in size gave prospects of speedier promotions.

Recruiting had been necessary almost all the time to keep the regiment up to the numerical standard; death and the discharge for disability had been operating from the first. It was now needful to fill it up to the artillery standard of eighteen hundred men, and this was successfully accomplished. Officers and men were despatched to Connecticut to gather recruits, and their advertisements set forth enticingly the advantage of joining a command so comfortably situated as "this famous regiment" in the Defences of Washington, where, it was permissible to infer, it was permanently stationed, a belief which had come to be generally held. The effort, however, was not confined by geographical limits, and a large part of the men secured were strangers to Litchfield County. Before the 1st of March, 1864, over eleven hundred recruits were received, and with the nucleus of the old regiment quickly formed into an efficient command.

"This vast body of recruits was made up of all sorts of men," the history of the regiment states. "A goodly portion of them were no less intelligent, patriotic, and honourable than the 'old' Nineteenth—and that is praise enough. Another portion of them were not exactly the worst kind of men, but those adventurous and uneasy varlets who always want to get out of jail when they are in, and in when they are out; furloughed sailors, for example, who had enlisted just for fun, while ashore, with

FORT ELLSWORTH, NEAR ALEXANDRIA, MAY, 1863

no definite purpose of remaining in the land service for any tedious length of time.

"And, lastly, there were about three hundred of the most thorough paced villains that the stews and slums of New York and Baltimore could furnish—bounty-jumpers, thieves, and cutthroats, who had deserted from regiment after regiment in which they had enlisted under fictitious names and who now proposed to repeat the operation. And they did repeat it. No less than two hundred and fifty deserted before the middle of May, very few of whom were ever retaken and returned to the regiment. There were rebels in Alexandria who furnished deserters with citizens' clothes and thus their capture became almost impossible."

At first, and perhaps to some extent always, there was a mental distinction made by the men between those who had originally enlisted in the "old Nineteenth," and the large body which was now joined to that organization, many of whom had never seen the Litchfield hills. But there was enough character in the original body to give its distinct tone to the enlarged regiment; its officers were all of the first enlistment, and the common sufferings and successes which soon fell to their lot quickly deprived this distinction of any invidiousness. The Second Artillery was always known, and proudly known, as the Litchfield County Regiment.

There came to the Second Connecticut Heavy Artillery, on May 17, 1864, the summons which, after such long immunity, it had almost ceased to expect.

The preceding two weeks had been among the most eventful of the war. They had seen the crossing of the Rapidan by Grant on the 4th, and the terrible battles for days following in the Wilderness and at Spottsylvania, depleting the army by such enormous losses as even this war had hardly seen before. Heavy reinforcements were demanded and sent forward from all branches of the service; in the emergency this artillery regiment was summoned to fight as infantry, and so served until the end of the conflict, though for a long time with a hope, which survived many disappointments, of being assigned to its proper work with the heavy guns.

It started for the front on May 18th (1864), and on the 20th reached the headquarters of the Army of the Potomac, and was assigned to the Second Brigade, First Division, of the Sixth Corps, now under Major-General Horatio G. Wright, another leader of Connecticut origin, who had succeeded to the command of the Corps on the death a few days before of Litchfield County's most noted soldier, John Sedgwick.

The famous series of movements "by the left flank" was in progress, and the regiment was in active motion at once. For more than a week following its arrival at the front it was on the march practically all the time while Grant pushed southward. To troops unaccustomed to anything more arduous than drilling in the Defences at Washington, it was almost beyond the limits of endurance. At the start, without experience in campaigning, the men had overburdened themselves with impedimenta which it was very soon necessary to dispense with.

"The amount of personal effects then thrown away," wrote the chaplain, Rev. Winthrop H. Phelps, "has been estimated by officers who witnessed and have carefully calculated it, to be from twenty to thirty thousand dollars. To this amount must be added the loss to the Government in the rations and ammunition left on the way."

On some of the marches days were passed with scarcely anything to eat, and it is recorded that raw corn was eagerly gathered, kernel by kernel, in empty granaries, and eaten with a relish. Heat, dust, rain, mud, and a rate of movement which taxed to the utmost the powers of the strongest, gave to these untried troops a savage hint of the hardships of campaigning, into which they had been plunged without any gradual steps of breaking in, and much more terrible experiences were close at hand.

Of these there came a slight foretaste in a skirmish with the enemy on the 24th near Jericho Ford on the North Anna River, resulting in the death of one man and the wounding of three others, the first of what was soon to be a portentous list of casualties.

The movements of both armies were bringing them steadily nearer to Richmond, and but one chance now remained to achieve the object of the campaign, the defeat of Lee's army north of the Chickahominy and away from the strong defences of the Confederate capital. The enemy, swinging southward to conform to Grant's advance, finally reached the important point of Cold Harbor on May 31st.

Cavalry was sent forward to dislodge him, and seized some of the entrenchments near that place, while both armies were hurried forward for the inevitable battle. The Sixth Corps, of which the Second Artillery was part, reached its position on the extreme left near noon

In the Defences. Guard mount

on June 1st, having marched since midnight, and awaited the placing of other troops before the charge, which had been ordered to take place at five o'clock.

It would have been a fearful waiting for these men could they have known what was in store for them. But they were drugged, as it were, with utter fatigue; the almost constant movement of their two weeks of active service had left them "so nearly dead with marching and want of sleep" that they could not notice or comprehend the significant movements of the columns of troops about them preparing for battle, or the artillery which soon opened fire on both sides; their stupor, it is related, was of a kind that none can describe.

They heard without excitement the earnest instructions of Colonel Kellogg, who, in pride and anxiety at this first trial of his beloved command, was in constant consultation with officers and men, directing, encouraging, explaining.

"He marked out on the ground," writes one of his staff, "the shape of the works to be taken,—told the officers what dispositions to make of the different battalions,—how the charge was to be made,—spoke of our reputation as a band-box regiment, 'Now we are called on to show what we can do at fighting.'"

The brigade commander, General Emory Upton, was also watching closely this new regiment which had never been in battle. But all foreboding was spared most of the men through sheer exhaustion.

At about the appointed time, five in the afternoon, the regiment was moved in three battalions of four companies each out of the breastworks where it had lain through the afternoon, leaving knapsacks behind, stationed for a few moments among the scanty pinewoods in front, and then at the word of command started forth upon its fateful journey, the Colonel in the lead.

The first battalion, with the colours in the centre, moved at a double quick across the open field under a constantly thickening fire, over the enemy's first line of rifle pits which was abandoned at its approach, and onward to the main line of breastworks with a force and impetus which would have carried it over this like Niagara but for an impassable obstruction.

Says the regimental history:

There had been a thick growth of pine sprouts and saplings on this ground, but the rebels had cut them, probably that very day, and had arranged them so as to form a very effective abatis,—

thereby clearing the spot and thus enabling them to see our movements. Up to this point there had been no firing sufficient to confuse or check the battalion, but here the rebel musketry opened. A sheet of flame, sudden as lightning, red as blood, and so near that it seemed to singe the men's faces, burst along the rebel breastwork, and the ground and trees close behind our line was ploughed and riddled with a thousand balls that just missed the heads of the men.

The battalion dropped flat on the ground, and the second volley, like the first, nearly all went over. Several men were struck, but not a large number. It is more than probable that if there had been no other than this front fire, the rebel breastworks would have been ours, notwithstanding the pine boughs. But at that moment a long line of rebels on our left, having nothing in their own front to engage their attention, and having unobstructed range on the battalion, opened a fire which no human valour could withstand, and which no pen can adequately describe.

It was the work of almost a single minute. The air was filled with sulphurous smoke, and the shrieks and howls of more than two hundred and fifty mangled men rose above the yells of triumphant rebels and the roar of their musketry. 'About face,' shouted Colonel Kellogg, but it was his last command. He had already been struck in the arm, and the words had scarcely passed his lips when another shot pierced his head, and he fell dead upon the interlacing pine boughs.

Wild and blind with wounds, bruises, noise, smoke, and conflicting orders, the men staggered in every direction, some of them falling upon the very top of the rebel parapet, where they were completely riddled with bullets,—others wandering off into the woods on the right and front, to find their way to death by starvation at Andersonville, or never to be heard of again.

The second battalion had advanced at an interval of about seventy-five yards after the first, and the third had followed in turn, but they were ordered by General Upton to lie down as they approached the entrenchments. They could not fire without injury to the line in front, and could only hold their dangerous and trying position in readiness to support their comrades ahead, protecting themselves as they could from the fire that seemed like leaden hail. There was no suggestion

GENERAL SEDGWICK

of retreat at any point and several hundred of the enemy, taking advantage of a lull in the firing, streamed over the breastworks and gave themselves up, but through a misunderstanding of the case the credit of their capture was given to other regiments, though clearly due to this.

The history continues:

The lines now became very much mixed. Those of the first battalion who were not killed or wounded gradually crawled or worked back; wounded men were carried through to the rear; and the woods began to grow dark, either with night or smoke or both. The companies were formed and brought up to the breastworks one by one, and the line extended toward the left. The enemy soon vacated the breastwork in our immediate front, and crept off through the darkness.

Throughout the terrible night they held their ground, keeping up a constant fire to prevent an attempt by the enemy to reoccupy the line, until they were relieved in the early morning by other troops; they had secured a position which it was indispensable to hold, and the line thus gained remained the regiment's front during its stay at Cold Harbor. Until June 12th the position was kept confronting the enemy, whose line was parallel and close before it, while daily additions were made to the list of casualties as they laboured in strengthening the protective works.

The official report of General Upton reads in part as follows:

The Second Connecticut, anxious to prove its courage, moved to the assault in beautiful order. Crossing an open field it entered a pine-wood, passed down a gentle declivity and up a slight ascent. Here the charge was checked. For seventy feet in front of the works the trees had been felled, interlocking with each other and barring all further advance. Two paths several yards apart, and wide enough for four men to march abreast, led through the obstruction. Up these to the foot of the works the brave men rushed but were swept away by a converging fire. Unable to carry the intrenchments, I directed the men to lie down and not return the fire. Opposite the right the works were carried. The regiment was marched to the point gained and, moving to the left, captured the point first attacked. In this position without support on either flank the Second Connecticut fought till three a.m., when the enemy fell back to a second line of works.

The regimental history continues:

On the morning of the 2nd the wounded who still remained were got off to the rear, and taken to the Division Hospital some two miles back. Many of them had lain all night, with shattered bones, or weak with loss of blood, calling vainly for help, or water, or death. Some of them lay in positions so exposed to the enemy's fire that they could not be reached until the breastworks had been built up and strengthened at certain points, nor even then without much ingenuity and much danger; but at length they were all removed. Where it could be done with safety, the dead were buried during the day. Most of the bodies, however, could not be reached until night, and were then gathered and buried under cover of the darkness.

The regiment's part in the charge of June 3rd, the disastrous movement of the whole Union line against the Confederate works, which Grant admitted never should have been made, was attended with casualties which by comparison with the slaughter of the 1st seemed inconsiderable. There were, in fact, losses in killed and wounded on almost all of the twelve days of its stay at Cold Harbor, but the fatal 1st of June greatly overshadowed the remaining time, and that first action was indeed incomparably the most severe the Second Connecticut ever saw. Its loss in killed and wounded, in fact, is said to have been greater than that of any other Connecticut regiment in any single battle.

The reputation of a fighting regiment, which its fallen leader had predicted, was amply earned by that unfaltering advance against intrenchments manned by Lee's veterans, and that tenacious defence of the position gained, but the cost was appallingly great. The record of Cold Harbor, of which all but a very small proportion was incurred on June 1st, is given as follows: Killed or died of wounds, one hundred and twenty-one; wounded, but not mortally, one hundred and ninety; missing, fifteen; prisoners, three.

General Martin T. McMahon, writing of this battle in *The Century's* series of war papers, says:

I remember at one point a mute and pathetic evidence of sterling valour. The Second Connecticut Heavy Artillery, a new regiment eighteen hundred strong, had joined us but a few days before the battle. Its uniform was bright and fresh; therefore its dead were easily distinguished where they lay. They marked in a dotted line an obtuse angle, covering a wide front, with its apex toward the enemy, and there upon his face, still in death, with his head to the works, lay the Colonel, the brave and genial Colonel Elisha S. Kellogg.

Such was their first trial in battle.

Immediately after receiving news of the action of June 1st, Governor Buckingham had sent a commission as colonel to Lieutenant-Colonel James Hubbard. He, however, was unwilling to assume the responsibility of the command; this had been his first battle, and he "drew the hasty inference that all the fighting was likely to consist of a similar walking into the jaws of hell. He afterwards found that this was a mistake."

Upon General Upton's advice, therefore, the officers recommended to the Governor the appointment of Ranald S. Mackenzie, then a captain of engineers on duty at headquarters, and this recommendation being favourably endorsed by superior officers up to the lieutenant-general, was accepted, and Colonel Mackenzie took command on June 6th.

Of the man who was now to lead the regiment, Grant in his *Memoirs* writes twenty years later the following unqualified judgment: "I regarded Mackenzie as the most promising young officer in the army. Graduating at West Point as he did during the second year of the war, he had won his way up to the command of a corps before its close. This he did upon his own merit and without influence." Such a statement from such a quarter is enough to show that once more the Second Connecticut was to be commanded by a soldier of more than ordinary qualities, a fact which was not long in developing.

Colonel Mackenzie's active connection with the regiment lasted only some four months, but they were months of great activity and afforded such occasions for proof of his abilities that his speedy promotion was inevitable. He never achieved the general popularity with his men that had come to his predecessor, nor cared to, but he did gain quite as thoroughly their respect through his mastership of the business in hand.

It was not long after he assumed command that, as the regimental history says, the men:

. . . .began to grieve anew over the loss of Kellogg. That commander had chastised us with whips, but this one dealt in scorpions. By the time we reached the Shenandoah Valley, he had so far developed as to be a far greater terror, to both officers and men, than Early's grape and canister. He was a Perpetual Punisher, and the Second Connecticut while under him was always a punished regiment. There is a regimental tradition to the effect that a well-defined purpose existed among the men, prior to the battle of Winchester, to dispose of this commanding scourge during the first fight that occurred.

If he had known it, it would only have excited his contempt, for he cared not a copper for the good will of any except his military superiors, and certainly feared no man of woman born, on either side of the lines. But the purpose, if any existed, quailed and failed before his audacious pluck on that bloody day. He seemed to court destruction all day long. With his hat aloft on the point of his sabre he galloped over forty-acre fields, through a perfect hailstorm of rebel lead and iron, with as much impunity as though he had been a ghost. The men hated him with the hate of hell, but they could not draw bead on so brave a man as that. Henceforth they firmly believed he bore a charmed life.

Colonel Mackenzie's advancement was brilliantly rapid, as Grant states, and at the time of Lee's surrender he was in command of a corps of cavalry, which had shortly before taken an important part in the battle of Five Forks under his leadership.

When the war ended he became colonel of the Twenty-fourth Infantry in the regular army, and later received a cavalry command, gaining much distinction by his services in the Indian campaigns in the West and on the Mexican border. He was made brigadier-general in 1882, shortly after placed on the retired list, and died at Governor's Island in 1889.

The unsuccessful assault on Lee's works at Cold Harbor marked the end of the first part of Grant's campaign. The next move was to swing the army southward to the line of the James River and prepare to move upon Richmond and its defences from that side. This change of base was one of General Grant's finest achievements, admirably planned, and so skilfully executed that for three days Lee remained in total ignorance of what his adversary was doing.

The Second Connecticut withdrew from its position on June 12th, late at night, reached the river on the 16th, and, moving up it in transports, was disembarked and sent toward Petersburg, to a point on the left wing of the army. It reached position on the night of the 19th and

THE FIRST BATTLE

entrenched. The usual occurrences of such marches as attended this change of scene were varied for the men, as the regimental history suggestively relates, by a notable circumstance—a bath in the river.

It was the only luxury we had had for weeks. It was a goodly sight to see half a dozen regiments disporting themselves in the tepid waters of the James. But no reader can possibly understand what enjoyment it afforded, unless he has slept on the ground for fourteen days without undressing, and been compelled to walk, cook, and live on all fours, lest a perpendicular assertion of his manhood should instantly convert it into clay.

The operations against Petersburg had been going on for some time when the regiment arrived, and for two days it lay in the rifle pits it had dug under continual fire, with frequent resulting casualties. It was:

the most intolerable position the regiment was ever required to hold. We had seen a deadlier spot at Cold Harbor, and others awaited us in the future; but they were agonies that did not last. Here, however, we had to stay, hour after hour, from before dawn until after dark, and that, too, where we could not move a rod without extreme danger. The enemy's line was parallel with ours, just across the wheat field; then they had numerous sharpshooters, who were familiar with every acre of the ground, perched in tall trees on both our flanks; then they had artillery posted everywhere.

No man could cast his eyes over the parapet, or expose himself ten feet in the rear of the trench without drawing fire. And yet they did thus expose themselves; for where there are even chances of being missed or hit, soldiers will take the chances rather than lie still and suffer from thirst, supineness, and want of all things. There was no getting to the rear until zigzag passages were dug, and then the wounded were borne off. Our occupation continued during the night and the next day, the regiment being divided into two reliefs, the one off duty lying a little to the rear, in a cornfield near Harrison's house. But it was a question whether 'off' or 'on' duty was the more dangerous.

On the 21st, relieved from this post, the regiment was moved to a new position further southwest and about the same distance from the city of Petersburg, which lay in plain view and whose city clocks could be heard distinctly. The Sixth Corps was engaged in an operation having the purpose of breaking Lee's communications with the South by the line of the Weldon Railroad, and in the course of this the Second Connecticut took part in a "sharp skirmish" with Hill's Division, on June 22nd, an affair which to other experiences would be notable as a battle of some proportions.

The desired result was not gained; the attempt on Petersburg, which if successful might have hastened the end of the Confederacy by six months, and which came so near success, was changed to besieging operations, and for some time Grant's army lay comparatively quiet. In its four days in action here, the regiment suffered as follows: Killed or died of wounds, fifteen; wounded but not mortally, fifteen; missing, three; prisoners who died, five.

On July 9th came the orders which took the Second Connecticut for many months away from its place before Petersburg, where, after the activities described, it had settled down to a less exciting course of constructing batteries, forts, and breastworks, and laying out camps, with days of comparative peace and comfort notwithstanding several alarms showing the possibility of more arduous service.

The Confederate Army which had been sent under General Early into the Shenandoah Valley to create a diversion in that quarter, had unexpectedly appeared on the Potomac in a sudden dash upon Washington, then defended chiefly by raw levies. Part of the Sixth Corps had been detached from Grant's army and sent to protect the capital a few days before; now the rest of the corps, including the Second Connecticut, was hurried north and reached Washington just in time to defeat Early's purpose. He had planned to storm the city on the 12th, and with good prospects of success; it was on that very day at an early hour, that the reinforcing troops arrived.

They were hurried through the city to the threatened point, and the enemy, seeing the well-known corps badge confronting them at Fort Stevens, and recognizing that the opportunity was gone, promptly retreated, after an engagement in which the Second Connecticut took no active part. This occasion was notable by reason of the fact that for the only time during the war President Lincoln was under fire, as he watched the progress of affairs from the parapet of Fort Stevens.

The pursuit which began at once entailed some hard marching, but the enemy could not be brought to a stand. It continued for several days until the Valley of the Shenandoah was reached, when Early, as was supposed, having hurried back to join Lee at Petersburg, the Sixth Corps was marched again swiftly to the capital. Here it developed that the authorities had decided to keep part of the forces sent for their protection, to man the defences, since Early's attempt had come so dangerously near succeeding, and the Second Connecticut was chosen to remain.

On July 25th it was moved into the same forts it had occupied when called to the front two months before, and here it might have remained through the rest of its term of service, if Early had, as was presumed, gone back to join Lee at Petersburg. But it was learned now that he had faced about when the chase ceased and was again threatening a northward move. The Sixth Corps was therefore ordered against his force once more, the Second Connecticut going from the anticipated comforts of its prospective garrison duty with anything but satisfaction.

The men who had rolled into those cosy bunks with the declared intention of 'sleeping a week steady,' were on their cursing way through Tenallytown again in twenty-four hours, marching with accelerated pace toward Frederick to overtake the brigade of the red cross, to which they had so lately bidden an everlasting *adieu*. Oh, bitter cup!

After much marching and counter marching they found themselves on August 6th at Halltown in the Valley. For more than a month the army, now placed under the command of General Sheridan, was occupied in organizing and manoeuvring for the projected campaign, which the presence of the hostile force in that important quarter necessitated.

Though on a much smaller scale than the operations in which the regiment had borne a part since it had been in active service, the impending action in the Shenandoah Valley was recognized as being of great importance. Grant's official report, speaking on this point, says: "Defeat to us would lay open to the enemy the states of Maryland and Pennsylvania for long distances before another army could be interposed to check him," and aside from the military aspect of the matter, the political campaign then agitating the loyal states made the result of the struggle here of profound influence.

The campaign's activities began with the battle of the Opequan, or, as it is perhaps more often designated, of Winchester. General Sheridan took advantage of an opportunity for which he had been patiently waiting by moving his forces to the attack at daylight on the morning of September 19th, and before noon the engagement was fierce and general, both assault and defence being made with equal spirit and determination; that part of the Sixth Corps which comprised the Second Connecticut, however, had taken small part in it, being held in reserve.

It was about midday that in a counter charge against the Union centre, the enemy found a weak point at the junction of the Sixth Corps with the Nineteenth, of which they quickly took advantage, breaking the line and driving back the troops on the flanks of both corps in great disorder. Their successful advance and the flight of the opposing forces gave such assurances of victory that more than one Confederate writer says that at this point the battle which had raged since daylight was won.

Jefferson Davis himself wrote, years after, of the charge: "This affair occurred about 11 a.m., and a splendid victory had been gained,"—a judgment which lacked finality. In fact, had the separation of the wings of Sheridan's army been accomplished, as it was threatened, the result would have been utter disaster; just now, however, Upton's brigade, of which the Second Connecticut formed a large part, was brought up to the point of danger. The charge was checked, the enemy in turn driven back, and the Union line re-established.

In the regimental history it is related that the brigade was pushed forward gradually:

. . halted on a spot where the ground was depressed enough to afford a little protection, and only a little,—for several men were hit while lying there, as well as others, while getting there. In three minutes the regiment again advanced, passed over a knoll, lost several more men, and halted in another hollow spot, similar to the first. The enemy's advance had now been pushed well back, and here a stay was made of perhaps two hours. Colonel Mackenzie rode slowly back and forth along the rise of ground in front of this position in a very reckless manner, in plain sight and easy range of the enemy, who kept up a fire from a piece of woods in front, which elicited from him the remark, 'I guess those fellows will get tired of firing at me by and by.' But the ground where the regiment lay was very slightly depressed, and although the shots missed Mackenzie they killed and wounded a large number of both officers and men behind him. About three o'clock, an advance of the whole line having been ordered by Sheridan, the regiment charged across the field,

Mackenzie riding some ten rods ahead, holding his hat aloft on the point of his sabre. The distance to the woods was at least a quarter of a mile, and was traversed under a fire that carried off its victims at nearly every step. The enemy abandoned the woods, however, as the regiment approached. After a short halt it again advanced to a rail fence which ran along the side of an extensive field.

Here, for the first time during the whole of this bloody day, did the regiment have orders to fire, and for ten minutes they had the privilege of pouring an effective fire into the rebels, who were thick in front. Then a flank movement was made along the fence to the right, followed by a direct advance of forty rods into the field. Here was the deadliest spot of the day.

The enemy's artillery, on a rise of ground in front, plowed the field with canister and shells, and tore the ranks in a frightful manner. Major Rice was struck by a shell, his left arm torn off, and his body cut almost asunder. Major Skinner was struck on the top of the head by a shell, knocked nearly a rod with his face to the earth, and was carried to the rear insensible. General Upton had a good quarter pound of flesh taken out of his thigh by a shell. Colonel Mackenzie's horse was cut in two by a solid shot which just grazed the rider's leg and let him down to the ground very abruptly.

Several other officers were also struck; and from these instances as well as from the appended list of casualties some idea may be gained of the havoc among the enlisted men at this point. Although the regiment had been under fire and losing continually from the middle of the afternoon, until it was now almost sunset, yet the losses during ten minutes in this last field were probably equal to those of all the rest of the day. It was doubtless the spot referred to by the rebel historian, Pollard, when he says, 'Early's artillery was fought to the muzzle of the guns.'

Mackenzie gave the order to move by the left flank and a start was made, but there was no enduring such a fire, and the men ran back and lay down. Another attempt was soon made, and after passing a large oak tree a sheltered position was secured. The next move was directly into the enemy's breastwork. They had just been driven from it by a cavalry charge from the right, and were in full retreat through the streets of Winchester, and some of their abandoned artillery which had done us so much damage stood yet in position, hissing hot with action, with their miserable rac-a-bone horses attached.

The brigade, numbering less than half the muskets it had in the morning, was now got into shape, and after marching to a field in the eastern edge of the city, bivouacked for the night, while the pursuit rolled miles away up the valley pike.

"Night alone," wrote General Wesley Merritt, "saved Early's army from capture."

To the losses of the day the Second Connecticut contributed forty-two killed and one hundred and eight wounded, the proportion of officers being very large.

Unlike their previous severe engagement at Cold Harbor, the regiment had the thrilling consciousness of complete victory to hearten them after this battle, and, later, when the full history of the day was learned, the realization that they had played a part of no little importance in attaining it.

The moment when they were brought into action was a critical one. General Sheridan, in his report summing up the operations of the campaign, said: "At Winchester for a moment the contest was uncertain, but the gallant attack of General Upton's brigade of the Sixth Corps restored the line of battle," and of this brigade the Second Connecticut formed fully half.

Upton's report gave high praise to Colonel Mackenzie, and said: "His regiment on the right initiated nearly every movement of the division, and behaved with great steadiness and gallantry."

The victory itself, with the sequel which followed so promptly three days later, had an importance far beyond its purely military value, through its marked effects upon public sentiment throughout the country; it brought to one side jubilant satisfaction, and gave a corresponding depression to the other, and it elevated Sheridan at once to that high place in popular affection which he always afterwards held. That it was "the turning-point of the fortunes of the war in Virginia," was the verdict of a Confederate officer of high rank, and Nicolay and Hay in the *Life of Lincoln* describe it as "one of the most important of the war."

As for the Litchfield County regiment, among its many proud memories, none surely holds a higher place than that of the worthy and effective part it took in this day's work, forming, as it did, so large a part of the brigade which, in the words of General Upton's biogra-

Colonel Wessells

pher, turned possible defeat into certain victory.

General Sheridan's method of operation could hardly be held as dilatory. It would doubtless have commended itself more highly to his men if it had been somewhat more so, when at daylight on the morning after the splendid success of September 19th they were ordered in pursuit of Early's army.

The Confederate forces had taken position on Fisher's Hill, considered the Gibraltar of the Valley, and according to Sheridan, almost impregnable to a direct assault. Two days were occupied in bringing up troops and making dispositions for the attack. The Second Connecticut reached its assigned position on the 21st near midnight, and found itself "on the very top of a hill fully as high as Fisher's Hill, and separated from it by Tumbling River. The enemy's stronghold was on the top of the opposite hill directly across the stream."

On the 22nd more or less skirmishing took place all day. A force had been sent round the enemy's left flank; the attack it delivered late in the afternoon was a complete surprise to Early's men, and an advance by the whole Union line quickly routed them.

To make this charge the regiment moved down the steep hill, waded the stream, and moved up the rocky front of the rebel Gibraltar. How they got up there is a mystery,—for the ascent of that rocky declivity would now seem an impossibility to an unburdened traveller, even though there were no deadly enemy at the top. But up they went, clinging to rocks and bushes. The main rebel breastwork, which they were so confident of holding, was about fifteen rods from the top of the bluff, with brush piled in front of it. Just as the top was reached the Eighth Corps struck the enemy on the right, and their flight was disordered and precipitate. The Second Connecticut was the first regiment that reached and planted colors on the works from the direct front.

They were marching in pursuit all that night and for three succeeding days, until the chase was seen to be hopeless and the army faced northward again. Four killed and nineteen wounded were added at Fisher's Hill to the growing record of the Second Connecticut's losses.

Such complete failure in their campaign had, it was now believed, eliminated the enemy in the Shenandoah Valley. The Sixth Corps was accordingly ordered back to Grant's army before Petersburg after a few days of rest, and was moving toward Washington on its way when there came a sudden change of orders.

Early, reinforced and once more ready, was again in the works he had been driven from at Fisher's Hill. The corps, recalled to join the forces of Sheridan, went into camp along the north bank of Cedar Creek on October 14th, and here there soon took place one of the most thrilling and dramatic conflicts of the war.

"For the next few days," the history of the regiment states, "there was much quiet and a good deal of speculation among the troops as to what would be the next shift of the scenes. The enemy was close in front, just as he had been for weeks preceding the battle of Winchester, but this attitude which might once have been called defiance, now seemed to be mere impudence,—and it was the general opinion that Early did not wish or intend to fight again, but that he was to be kept there as a standing threat in order to prevent Sheridan's army from returning to Grant. And yet there was something mysterious in his conduct. He was known to be receiving reinforcements, and his signal flags on Three-top Mountain (just south of Fisher's Hill) were continually in motion. From the top of Massanutton Mountain his *vedettes* could look down upon the whole Union army, as one can look down upon New Haven from East Rock, and there is no doubt that the exact location of every camp, and the position of every gun and every picket post were thoroughly known to him. Nevertheless, it seemed the most improbable thing in the world that he could be meditating either an open attack or a surprise. The position was strong, the creek and its crossings in possession of our pickets both along the front and well out on either flank."

But Early himself, being in difficulties his enemy knew nothing of, says, "I was compelled to move back for want of provisions and forage, or attack the enemy in his position with the hope of driving him from it, and I determined to attack."

His plan was, like his adversary's at the last encounter, a surprise around the left flank with a feint on the right, and it was carried out on the morning of October 19th with complete success. General Sheridan had been called to Washington a few days before, as no active operations seemed imminent, and the army lay feeling quite secure.

Good fortune attended the attacking forces, and the surprise was perfect. General Merritt writes:

Crook's (Eighth Corps) camp and afterwards Emory's (Nineteenth Corps) were attacked in flank and rear, and the men and officers driven from their beds, many of them not having time to hurry into their clothes, except as they retreated, half awake and terror-stricken from the overpowering numbers of the enemy. Their own artillery in conjunction with that of the enemy, was turned on them, and long before it was light enough for their eyes, unaccustomed to the dim light, to distinguish friend from foe, they were hurrying to our right and rear intent only on their safety. Wright's (Sixth Corps) infantry, which was farther removed from the point of attack, fared somewhat better, but did not offer more than a spasmodic resistance.

Nevertheless, they made Early "pay dearly for every foot gained and finally brought him to a stand," as Nicolay and Hay record.

The history of the Second Connecticut tells the story of the day as follows:

Most of the regiment were up next morning long before Reveille and many had begun to cook their coffee on account of that ominous popping and cracking which had been going on for half an hour off to the right. They did not exactly suppose it meant anything, but they had learned wisdom by many a sudden march on an empty stomach and did not propose to be caught napping. The clatter on the right increased. It began to be the wonder why no orders came. But suddenly every man seemed to lose interest in the right, and turned his inquiring eyes and ears toward the left. Rapid volleys and a vague tumult told that there was trouble there. 'Fall in!' said Mackenzie.

The brigade moved briskly off toward the east, crossing the track of other troops and batteries of artillery which were hurriedly swinging into position, while ambulances, orderlies, staff officers, camp followers, pack horses, cavalrymen, sutler's wagons, hospital wagons, and six-mule teams of every description came trundling and galloping pell-mell toward the right and rear and making off toward Winchester. It was not a hundred rods from our own camp to the place where we went into position on a road running north.

General Wright, the temporary commander of the army, bareheaded, and with blood trickling from his beard, sat on his horse nearby, as if bewildered or in a brown study. The ground was cleared in front of the road and sloped off some thirty rods to a stream, on the opposite side of which it rose for about an equal distance to a piece of woods in which the advance rebel line had already taken position. The newly risen sun, huge and bloody, was on their side in more senses than one. Our line faced directly to the east and we could see nothing but that enormous disk, rising out of the fog, while they could see every man in our line and could take good aim.

The battalion lay down, and part of the men began to fire, but the shape of the ground afforded little protection and large numbers were killed and wounded. Four fifths of our loss for the entire day occurred during the time we lay here,—which could not have been over five minutes,—by the end of which time the Second Connecticut found itself in an isolated position not unlike that at Cold Harbor. The fog had now thinned away somewhat and a firm rebel line with colours full high advanced came rolling over the knoll just in front of our left not more than three hundred yards distant. 'Rise up,—Retreat,' said Mackenzie,—and the battalion began to move back.

For a little distance the retreat was made in very good order, but it soon degenerated into a rout. Men from a score of regiments were mixed up in flight, and the whole corps was scattered over acres and acres with no more organization than a herd of buffaloes. Some of the wounded were carried for a distance by their comrades, who were at length compelled to leave them to their fate in order to escape being shot. About a mile from the place where the retreat commenced there was a road running directly across the valley. Here the troops were rallied and a slight defence of rails thrown up.

The regimental and brigade flags were set up as beacons to direct each man how to steer through the mob and in a very few minutes there was an effective line of battle established. A few round shot ricocheted overhead, making about an eighth of a mile at a jump, and a few grape were dropped into a ditch just behind our line, quickly clearing out some soldiers who had crawled in there, but this was the extent of the pursuit. The whole brigade (and a very small brigade it was) was deployed as skirmishers under Colonel Olcott of the One Hundred and Twenty-first New York.

Three lines of skirmishers were formed and each in turn constituted the first line while the other two passed through and halted, and so the retreat was continued for about three miles until a halt was made upon high ground, from which we could plainly see the Johnnies sauntering around on the very ground where we had slept."

Once more could Early claim the credit of a victory of which at night he was to find himself again deprived. Sheridan's famous ride, his meeting and turning of the tide of fugitives, is the feature of the day's occurrences which will always live in the popular memory. It is a significant hint of the scale of such a battlefield to know that the men of the Second Connecticut had no visual perception of his presence that day, though they heard the cheering occasioned by his appearance in other parts of the scene, and in his report there is mention of a meeting with Colonel Mackenzie, whom he tried to persuade to go to the rear on account of his wounds.

The Confederate belief in their victory was not unreasonable, but it was now to suffer an astonishing upset. Weary and demoralized with success, they were entirely unprepared for the vigour of their opponents, who after repulsing their last assault, quickly reformed the lines and prepared for a general advance. Sheridan writes: "This attack was brilliantly made, and as the enemy was protected by rail breastworks and at some portions of his line by stone fences, his resistance was very determined."

The history of the Second Connecticut gives a detailed account of its movement, first against a stone wall in front which after some opposition was abandoned by the enemy, who then:

. . . .attempted to rally behind another fence a little further back, but after a moment or two gave it up and 'retired.' Not only in front of our regiment, but all along as far as the eye could reach, both to the right and left, were they flying over the uneven country in precisely the same kind of disorder that we had exhibited in the morning. The shouts and screams of victory mingled with the roar of the firing, and never was heard 'so musical a discord, such sweet thunder.' The sight of so many rebel heels made it a very easy thing to be brave, and the Union troops pressed on, utterly regardless of the grape and canister which to the last moment the enemy flung behind him.

It would not have been well for them to have fired too much if they had had ever so good a chance, for they would have been no more likely to hit our men than their own, who were our prisoners and scattered in squads of twenty, squads of ten, and squads of one, all over the vast field. At one time they made a determined stand along a ridge in front of our brigade.

A breastwork of rails was thrown together, colours planted, a nucleus made, and both flanks grew longer and longer with wonderful rapidity. It was evident that they were driving back their men to this line without regard to regiment or organization of any kind. This could be plainly seen from the adjacent and similar ridge over which we were moving,—the pursuers being in quite as much disorder (so far as organizations were concerned) as the pursued. That growing line began to look ugly and somewhat quenched the ardour of the chase.

It began to be a question in many minds whether it would not be a point of wisdom 'to survey the vantage of the ground' before getting much further. But just as we descended into the intervening hollow, a body of cavalry, not large but compact, was seen scouring along the fields to our right and front like a whirlwind directly toward the left flank of that formidable line on the hill. When we reached the top there was no enemy there! They had moved on and the cavalry after them.

Thus the chase was continued, from position to position, for miles and miles, for hours and hours, until darkness closed in and every regiment went into camp on the identical ground it had left in such haste in the morning. Every man tied his shelter tent to the very same old stakes, and in half an hour coffee was boiling and salt pork sputtering over thousands of camp fires. Civil life may furnish better fare than the army at Cedar Creek had that night, but not better appetites; for it must be borne in mind that many had gone into the fight directly from their beds and had eaten nothing for twenty-four hours.

Men from every company started out the first thing after reaching camp to look for our dead and wounded, many of whom lay not fifty rods off. The slightly wounded who had not got away had been taken prisoners and sent at once toward Richmond—while the severely wounded had lain all day on the ground near where they were hit while the tide of battle ebbed and flowed over them.

Some of the mortally wounded were just able to greet their returning comrades, hear the news of victory, and send a last message to their friends before expiring. Corporal Charles M. Burr

COLONEL KELLOGG

was shot above the ankle just after the battalion had risen up and started to retreat. Both bones of his leg were shattered and he had to be left. In a few minutes the rebel battalion which I have already mentioned came directly over him in pursuit, and was soon out of his sight. Then being alone for a short time he pulled off the boot from his sound leg, put his watch and money into it and put it on again.

Next a merciful rebel lieutenant came and tied a handkerchief around his leg, stanching the blood. Next came the noble army of stragglers and bummers with the question, 'Hello, Yank, have you got any Yankee notions about you?' and at the same time thrusting their hands into every pocket. They captured a little money and small traps, but seeing one boot was spoiled they did not meddle with the other. Next came wagons, picking up muskets and accoutrements which lay thick all over the ground.

Then came ambulances and picked up the rebel wounded but left ours. Then came a citizen of the Confederacy asking many questions, and then came three boys who gave him water. And thus the day wore along until the middle of the afternoon when the tide of travel began to turn. The noble army of stragglers and bummers led the advance—then the roar of battle grew nearer and louder and more general, then came galloping officers and all kinds of wagons, then a brass twelve-pounder swung round close to him, unlimbered, fired one shot, and whipped off again—then came the routed infantry, artillery, and cavalry, all mixed together, all on a full run, and strewing the ground with muskets and equipments.

Then came the shouting 'boys in blue,' and in a few minutes Pat Birmingham came up and said: 'Well, Charley, I'm glad to find you alive. I didn't expect it. We're back again in the old camp, and the Johnnies are whipped all to pieces.'

The victory was as complete and satisfying as it was spectacular; the enemy was at last so thoroughly beaten that a dangerous attitude could not be taken again. It was a fitting close for Sheridan's famous campaign in the Shenandoah Valley.

To the Second Connecticut the day at Cedar Creek brought losses nearly as heavy as were suffered at Winchester just a month before: thirty-eight killed, ninety-six wounded, and two missing, besides a large number made prisoners,—an entire company having been captured early in the morning while on picket,—of whom eleven died in captivity. These losses were in fact proportionately even larger than those met with at Cold Harbor, as the hard service of the preceding months had reduced the regiment's effective strength to about twenty-five officers and seven hundred men present for duty.

General Sheridan's report on the Shenandoah campaign gave high praise to Colonel Mackenzie, who, as a result of his conduct, received a promotion and was commissioned brigadier-general in December. His disability from the two wounds received at Cedar Creek, however, necessitated his relinquishing the command of the regiment immediately after that engagement, and this devolved upon Lieutenant-Colonel James Hubbard; to him in due course came the colonel's commission, and he led the regiment throughout the rest of its career.

Colonel Hubbard, though born in Salisbury, had lived in the West before the war, and first saw service with an Illinois regiment. Returning to Connecticut, he assisted in raising a company for the Nineteenth, and was mustered in as its captain. He was steadily promoted until the death of Colonel Kellogg brought him naturally to the command of the regiment; but, as has been said, his own modest estimate of his qualifications for this responsibility caused him to decline the appointment. When it came to him a second time he accepted, and proved by his subsequent handling of the regiment a worthy successor to the remarkably able soldiers under whom he had served, winning the brevet rank of brigadier-general in the final campaigns. His ambition was, a comrade wrote, to do his full duty without a thought for personal glory; and he enjoyed in a high degree the respect and affection of his command. He died in Washington, where he lived for many years, on December 21, 1886, and was buried in Winsted.

The brilliant victories in which the Second Artillery had borne so worthy a part, and the re-election of President Lincoln in November (1864), put an end to all anxieties as to danger in the quarter of the Shenandoah, which before Sheridan's campaign had been a region of fatal mischance to the national cause from the beginning of the war. As a consequence the Sixth Corps was once more ordered to rejoin Grant's army, and the regiment left the historic valley on December 1st, arriving on the 5th before Petersburg, where it was assigned a position near the place of its skirmish on June 22nd.

"Then it was unbroken forest," says its history; "now, hundreds of acres were cleared, and dotted with camps. A corduroy road ran by, and a telegraph, and Grant's railroad. No other such railroad was ever seen before, or ever will be again. It was laid right on top of the ground, without any attempt at grading, and you might see the engine and rear car of a long train, while the middle of the train would be in a valley, completely out of sight. Having reached Parke Station, we moved to a camp near Battery Number Twenty-seven, and went into the snug and elegant little log houses just vacated by the Ninety-fourth New York. This was a new kind of situation for the 'Second Heavies.' The idea of being behind permanent and powerful breastworks, defended by abatis, ditches, and what not, with approaches so difficult that ten men could hold five hundred at bay, was so novel, that the men actually felt as if there must be some mistake, and that they had got into the wrong place."

For two months no fighting fell to the regiment's lot, for though the Union commanders and armies were ready and eager to make an end of the war as soon as possible, little could be done during the winter. Though this inactivity brought perhaps some relief from the rigors of army life, the men had numerous reminders that they were still in active service. One of the chief events of this season the history of the regiment describes as follows:

On the afternoon of the 9th (December, 1864), the First and Third Divisions of the Sixth Corps were marched to the left, beyond the permanent lines, and off in the direction of the Weldon Railroad, to prevent any attack on the Fifth and Second Corps, now returning from their expedition. After going for about six miles we halted for the night, in a piece of woods. It was bitter cold when we left camp, but soon began to moderate, then to rain, then to sleet; so that by the time we halted, everything was covered with ice, with snow two inches deep on the ground, and still sifting down through the pines.

It was the work of an hour to get fires going,—but at last they began to take hold, and fuel was piled on as though it did not cost anything. Clouds of steam rolled out of the soaked garments of the men, as they stood huddled around the roaring, cracking piles,—and the black night and ghostly woods were lighted up in a style most wonderful. The storm continued all night, and many a man waked up next morning to find his legs firmly packed in new fallen snow. At daylight orders came to pack up and be ready to move at once; which was now a difficult order to execute, on account of many things, especially the shelter tents;—for they were as rigid as sheet-iron and yet had to be rolled up and strapped on the knapsacks.

Nevertheless it was not long before the regiment was in motion; and after plodding off for a mile to the left, a line of battle was formed, *vedettes* sent out, trees felled and breastworks built, and at dinner-time the men were allowed to build fires and cook breakfast. Then, after standing until almost night in the snow, which had now turned to sleet, the column was headed homeward.

Upon arriving, it was discovered that some of the Jersey Brigade had taken possession of our log snuggeries, and that their officers had established their heels upon the mantels in our officers' quarters, and were smoking the pipes of comfort and complacency, as though they had not a trouble in the world, and never expected to have. But they soon found that possession is not nine points of military law, by any means. An order from Division Headquarters soon sent them profanely packing,—and the Second Heavies occupied.

Though weeks were spent in such comparative comfort and immunity as the present situation afforded, the men felt as if they were resting over a volcano which might break into fierce activity at any moment; and as the winter passed signs of the renewal of the struggle multiplied on all sides.

On February 5th (1865), part of the Second Connecticut was ordered to move out to support and protect the flank of the Fifth Corps, which was engaged near Hatcher's Run, and accordingly left the comforts of the camp and bivouacked for the night a few miles away. The history of the regiment says:

It was bitter cold sleeping that night—so cold that half the men stood or sat around fires all night. In the morning the movement was continued.

A little before sundown we crossed Hatcher's Run and moved by the flank directly into a piece of woods, the Second Brigade under Hubbard leading the division and the Second Connecticut under Skinner leading the brigade. Wounded men were being brought to the rear and the noise just ahead told of mischief there. Colonel Hubbard filed to the left at the head of the column along a slight ridge and about half the regiment had filed when troops of the Fifth Corps came running through to the rear and at the same moment General Wheaton rode up with 'oblique to the left, oblique to the left,' and making energetic gestures toward the rise of ground.

The ridge was quickly gained and fire opened just in time to head off a counter fire and charge that was already in progress, but between the 'file left' and the 'left oblique' and the breaking of our ranks by troops retreating from in front, and the vines and underbrush (which were so thick that they unhorsed some of the staff officers) there was a good deal of confusion, and the line soon fell back about ten rods, where it was reformed and a vigorous fire poured—somewhat at random—a little to the left of our first position.

The attempt of the enemy to get in on the left of the Fifth Corps was frustrated. Our casualties were six wounded (some of them probably by our own men) and one missing. The position was occupied that night, and the next day until about sundown, when the brigade shifted some distance to the right and again advanced under an artillery fire to within a short distance of the rebel batteries and built breastworks. The rebel picket shots whistled overhead all the time the breastworks were building, but mostly too high to hurt anything but the trees.

At midnight the division moved back to quarters, arriving at sunrise. Having taken a ration of whiskey which was ordered by Grant or somebody else in consideration of three nights and two days on the bare ground in February, together with some fighting and a good deal of hard marching and hard work, the men lay down to sleep as the sun rose up, and did not rise up until the sun went down.

The routine of picket duty, inspection, alarms, and orders to be in readiness which came not infrequently, continued for another succession of weeks, varied now by the constant arrival of deserters from the enemy, who were coming into the Union lines singly and in large parties almost daily, and revealing the desperate condition on the other side. Preparations went on for what all felt was to be the final campaign; and this opened for the Second Connecticut on March 25th, when the famous assault on Fort Stedman was made by the enemy, Lee's last attempt at offensive operations.

This position, which was on the eastern side of the city of Petersburg, was gallantly attacked and captured in the early morning; troops were at once called from all parts of the Union line and hurried to the point of action, but the fort was retaken before the Second Connecticut reached the scene, and the regiment was then moved to the southwest of the city before Fort Fisher, a general assault of the whole extensive line having been ordered by Grant to develop the weakness that Lee must have been obliged to make somewhere to carry out his plan against Fort Stedman. The attack succeeded in gaining and holding a large share of the Confederate picket line, a matter of great importance.

The Second Connecticut advanced to the charge late in the afternoon "as steadily as though on a battalion drill," the regimental history relates. It captured a line of rifle pits and kept on:

.... under a combined artillery and musket fire. The air was blue with the little cast iron balls from spherical-case shot which shaved the ground and exploded among the stumps just in rear of the line at intervals of only a few seconds. Twenty of the Second Connecticut were wounded—seven of them mortally—in reaching, occupying, and abandoning this position, which, proving entirely untenable, was held only a few minutes.

The line faced about and moved back under the same mixed fire of solid shot, spherical case, and musketry, and halted not far in front of the spot whence it had first moved forward. Other troops on the right now engaged the battery and captured the rest of the picket line, and after half an hour the brigade again moved forward to a position still further advanced than the previous one, where a permanent picket line was established.

The week following this eventful day, which began with the capture of one of the Union works, and ended with substantial gains along their front, saw intense activity on all sides. The abandonment of Petersburg by Lee was now plainly imminent, and the preventing of his army's escape was the paramount object. The whole vast field of operation about the besieged city became a seething theatre of complicated movement, and the Second Connecticut, under frequent orders for immediate advance, was formed in line at all hours of the day or night, and excited by a thousand rumours and orders given and revoked, but it did not finally leave its quarters during this time.

On April 1st, Sheridan won his notable victory at Five Forks, and at midnight the regiment was ordered out for a final charge on the defences so long held against them, which was to be made early on the

2nd. All was made ready, the lines formed, and at daylight the signal gun set the army in motion.

The advance was over precisely the same ground as on the 25th of March, and the firing came from the same battery and breastworks, although not quite so severe. Lieutenant-Colonel Skinner and seven enlisted men were wounded—none of them fatally. There was but little firing on our side, but with bayonets fixed the boys went in,—not in a very mathematical right line, but strongly and surely,—on, on, until the first line was carried. Then, invigorated and greatly encouraged by success, they pressed on—the opposing fire slackening every minute,—on, on, through the abatis and ditch, up the steep bank, over the parapet into the rebel camp that had but just been deserted. Then and there the long tried and ever faithful soldiers of the Republic saw daylight—and such a shout as tore the concave of that morning sky it were worth dying to hear.

The same jubilant success was attending the whole army, though not without sharp resistance on the part of the enemy in places.

Throughout the day advances were made and the works so long besieged were occupied all over the vast field, and at night the men "lay down in muddy trenches, among the dying and the dead, under a most murderous fire of sharpshooters. There had been charges and counter charges,—but our troops held all they had gained. At length the hot day gave place to chilly night, and the extreme change brought much suffering. The men had flung away whatever was fling-away-able during the charge of the morning and the subsequent hot march—as men always will, under like circumstances—and now they found themselves blanketless, stockingless, overcoatless,—in cold and damp trenches, and compelled by the steady firing to lie still, or adopt a horizontal, crawling mode of locomotion, which did not admit of speed enough to quicken the circulation of the blood. Some took clothing from the dead and wrapped themselves in it; others, who were fortunate enough to procure spades, dug gopher holes, and burrowed.

At daylight the Sixty-fifth New York clambered over the huge earthwork, took possession of Fort Hell, opened a picket fire and fired one of the guns in the fort, eliciting no reply. Just then a huge fire in the direction of the city, followed by several explosions, convinced our side that Lee's army had indeed left. The regiment was hastily got together,—ninety muskets being all that could be produced,—and sent out on picket. The picket line advanced and meeting with no resistance pushed on into the city. What regiment was first to enter the city is and probably ever will be a disputed question.

The Second Connecticut claims to have been in first, but Colonel Hubbard had ordered the colors to remain behind when the regiment went out on the skirmish line, consequently the stars and stripes that first floated over captured Petersburg belonged to some other regiment. Colonel Hubbard was, however, made Provost-Marshal of the city, and for a brief while dispensed government and law in that capacity."

Petersburg, however, now that it was abandoned by the enemy, had lost the importance it had so long possessed, and all energies were given to preventing the escape of its late defenders. Before the end of the day (April 3rd) the regiment, with the rest of the Sixth Corps, had turned westward and joined the pursuit. The chase was stern and the marches rapid, but far less wearing to these victorious veterans, filled with the consciousness of success, than those that had initiated their campaigning less than a year before.

On April 6th the regiment, after an all day march, came up with the enemy in position at Sailor's Creek, and went into the last engagement of its career. It was a charge under a hot fire, sharp and decisive, which quickly changed to a pursuit of the fleeing enemy, kept up until the bivouac at ten o'clock. The Second Connecticut captured the headquarters train of General Mahone, a battle flag, and many prisoners, and ended the tale of its losses with three men killed and six wounded.

The chase was taken up next morning (April 7th), and the regiment had reached a point close to Appomattox Court House, when on April 9th Lee met Grant and surrendered what remained of his army, at that historic place.

To imagine all that this meant to the men in arms is far easier than to attempt its description. They saw at last the end arriving of all the privation and suffering they had volunteered to undergo; they saw the triumph of the Union they had risen to defend to the uttermost extremity a proven fact. The whole continent vibrated with the deepest feeling at the news of it, but they, better than any others, knew in the fullest degree its immense significance.

Immediately after the surrender of the Army of Northern Virginia, the Sixth Corps was moved to Burkesville, some distance from Ap-

COLONEL MACKENZIE

pomattox in the direction of Richmond, and there it remained for about ten days awaiting events. On April 22nd it was ordered southward to Danville, with a view to joining Sherman's army then confronting Johnston in North Carolina, a movement which again necessitated some fatiguing marches, the one hundred and five miles being covered in less than five days.

News was received, however, that Johnston had followed the example of Lee and surrendered, and the corps thereupon faced about once more. On its leisurely progress to the north it was joined by crowds of the newly freed negroes, who attached themselves to every regiment in droves, and the lately hostile inhabitants came also at every stopping place, "with baskets and two-wheeled carts" for supplies to relieve their dire necessities.

Near Richmond the regiment remained several days, and the men were allowed passes to visit the late Confederate capital, so long the goal of their strenuous efforts.

The burnt district was still smoking with the remains of the great fire of April 2nd, and the city was full of officers and soldiers of the ex-Confederate army. The blue and the gray mingled on the streets and public squares, and were seen side by side in the Sabbath congregations. The war was over.

The consciousness of this last great fact was now becoming insistent in the minds of these citizen soldiers. The great purpose for which they had offered themselves was carried out, and their eagerness to have done with all the circumstances of military life was increasingly strong, and grew so intense as to render the final weeks of their term of service extremely trying.

The tremendous task of disbanding the armies of the Union was occupying the entire energies of the War Department, but to the men it seemed as if their longed for turn would never come. Back in the well-known fortifications around Washington they waited, taking part in the Grand Review on June 8th, in all the misery of full dress, and in a temper that would have carried them against the thousands of acclaiming spectators with savage joy, had it been a host of enemies in arms.

But their turn came at last, and on July 7th, one hundred and eighty-three men, all that were left of the original enlisted men of the "old Nineteenth," were mustered out; two days later they departed for New Haven and were welcomed there, like all the returning troops, with patriotic rejoicing.

The remainder of the regiment, some four hundred in number, was mustered out in its turn on August 18th, reached New Haven on the 20th, and:

> ... passed up Chapel Street amid welcoming crowds of people, the clangour of bells, and a shower of rockets and red lights that made the field-and-staff horses prance with the belief that battle had come again. After partaking of a bounteous entertainment prepared in the basement of the State House, the regiment proceeded to Grapevine Point, where, on the 5th of September, they received their pay and discharge, and the Second Connecticut Heavy Artillery vanished from sight and passed into History.

In Litchfield County the return of the various contingents to their homes was made the occasion of great rejoicing. Chief among these celebrations was a grand reception at the county seat on August 1st, when the first detachment to be discharged had arrived; they were *fêted* with dinner and speeches, illuminations and a triumphal arch. There were also other organized demonstrations in other towns, and everywhere the strongest manifestations of pride in these warrior sons of the county, and joy at their return.

But all who went had not returned. The terrible significance of the cold and formal columns and tables of the regiment's casualties was felt in every town, and to their tale was added in succeeding years a long list of the many who had indeed come back, but broken with wounds and disease, and just as truly devoted to death through their service as those who fell upon the field of battle.

What the Second Connecticut suffered is shown, so far as official statistics go, in the tables published by the Adjutant-General of the state, as follows:

Killed	147
Missing in action, probably killed	11
Fatally wounded	95
Wounded	427
Captured	72
Died in prison	21
Died of disease or accident	154
Discharged for disability	285
Unaccounted for at muster out	35

The officers of the regiment as mustered out were: Colonel, James Hubbard, Salisbury; lieutenant-colonel, Jeffrey Skinner, Winchester; majors, Edward W. Jones, New Hartford; Augustus H. Fenn, Plymouth; Chester D. Cleveland, Barkhamsted; adjutant, Theodore F. Vaill, Litchfield; quartermaster, Edward C. Huxley, Goshen; surgeon, Henry Plumb, New Milford; assistant surgeons, Robert G. Hazzard, New Haven; Judson B. Andrews, New Haven; chaplain, Winthrop H. Phelps, Barkhamsted.

The preceding pages have outlined the career of the Second Connecticut Heavy Artillery, and have narrated some of the more memorable events of its history. Enough has been told of what it did to furnish grounds for deducing what it was; but to deal with the regiment on the personal side is hardly possible within the limits of such a sketch as this, though it is a matter that cannot be entirely passed by. It need not be said that there is abundant human interest attaching as a matter of course to such men as were in the aggregate the subjects of so fine a record.

Any body of men—a college class, a legislature, a regiment—is in character what its component members make it; in this case there was the material, which, furnished with worthy leadership—and it unquestionably had that—made up the organization whose not uneventful existence has been described.

That they were better men, or worse, braver men, or more patriotic, than their descendants and successors would prove under similar conditions, or than the hundreds of thousands of their contemporaries who devoted themselves to the same service, is not to be believed; yet to have passed through such experiences as have been recounted, which became for them for a time the commonplaces of everyday life, is enough to place them apart from ordinary men in the eyes of our peace knowing generation. In fact, to have passed the tests of so fierce a course of education gives them a title to a place thus apart.

The university man of today, as the burden of the baccalaureate sermons so frequently testifies, is consigned to a special place of responsibility in life because of his training; these men surely earned one of special honour by reason of theirs, which was, too, not like the other, preparation alone, but also fulfilment. The realization of how typical it all was of that generation and that time, brings the clearest understanding of the real scope of the Civil War.

To the members of the Litchfield County University Club it is perhaps a point of interest to take brief notice of those names on the regimental rolls which would probably have been found upon its list of members had the organization been in existence in that earlier time. A number of the officers and men were college graduates when they enlisted, and others gained degrees after the war ended; the list which follows is, however, necessarily incomplete; in fact, an absolutely correct list is no doubt hopelessly impossible.

Major James Q. Rice, who was killed at Winchester, was a member of the class of 1850 at Wesleyan, and received from that institution the degree of Master of Arts in 1855. At the time of the regiment's formation he was conducting an academy in Goshen, and was enlisted as captain of a company which he had been active in recruiting.

Lieutenant-Colonel Nathaniel Smith of Woodbury entered the Yale Law School in the class of 1853, but did not graduate. Ill health forced him to relinquish his commission early in 1864, and until his death in 1877 he was a leading citizen of the county.

Judge Augustus H. Fenn, Major and Brevet-Colonel, came back from the war, having lost an arm at Cedar Creek, to take a course in the Law School at Harvard, and Yale made him a Master of Arts in 1889. His prominence for many years in public life and as judge in the highest courts in the state is well known. At the time of his death in 1897, he was a lecturer in the Yale Law School, and member of the Supreme Court of Errors.

Rev. James Deane, Captain and Brevet-Major, was a graduate of Williams in the class of 1857. He was pastor of the Congregational church at East Canaan when the regiment was organized, and was one of its recruiting officers.

Adjutant Theodore F. Vaill, the historian of the regiment, was a student before the war at Union College, but did not graduate.

Captain George S. Williams, of New Milford, was a member of the class of 1852 at Yale for a time, and received a degree from Trinity in 1855.

Surgeon Henry Plumb, and Assistant-Surgeons Robert G. Hazzard and John W. Lawton were all graduates of the Yale Medical School, in the classes of 1861, 1862, and 1859. Assistant-Surgeon Judson B. Andrews graduated at Yale in 1855. He was captain in a New York regiment in the early part of the war, and became afterward superintendent of the Buffalo State Hospital, and a recognized authority on insanity before his death in 1894.

Colonel Hubbard

Chaplain Jonathan A. Wainwright graduated at the University of Vermont in 1846, and after the war was for some years rector of St. John's Church in Salisbury. He was later connected with a church college in Missouri, where he died in 1898.

Captain William H. Lewis, Jr., studied after the war at the Berkeley Divinity School, and has been for many years rector of St. John's Church in Bridgeport.

Lieutenant and Brevet-Captain Lewis W. Munger, graduating at Brown in 1869 and later from the Crozier Theological Seminary, entered the ministry of the Baptist church.

Corporal Francis J. Young entered the Yale Medical School before the war, and returned after its close to take his degree in 1866.

Hospital Steward James J. Averill also graduated at the Yale Medical School after the war.

Sergeant Theodore C. Glazier was a graduate of Trinity in the class of 1860, and was a tutor there when he enlisted. He was later made colonel of a coloured regiment, and served with credit in that capacity.

Corporal Edward C. Hopson, a graduate of Trinity in 1864, was killed at Cedar Creek.

Sergeant Garwood R. Merwin, who had been a member of the class of 1864 at Yale, died at Alexandria in 1863.

Sergeant Romulus C. Loveridge, who had been entered in the class of 1865 at Yale, received a commission in a colored regiment.

Colonel Mackenzie graduated at West Point in 1862, but he was never a resident of the county, or of Connecticut, and his only connection with either was through his commission from Governor Buckingham.

There are not a few other names upon the rolls of the regiment which upon more thorough investigation than has been possible in the present case would certainly be added to the list. A complete history of the organization would also give a large place to the association of its veterans formed shortly after the war, whose frequent gatherings have more than a superficial likeness to the reunions of college classes. Memorable among these meetings was the one held on October 21, 1896, the occasion being the dedication of the regiment's monument in the National Cemetery at Arlington, with a pilgrimage also to the scenes of its battles and marches in the Shenandoah Valley nearby.

As a whole, the regiment was a body thoroughly representative not only of the army of which it was a fraction, an army as has been often said unlike any other the world has known, but also of the population from which it was drawn. It was made up of men of almost all conditions of life and of widely different ages, though naturally with young men in a large majority; of mechanics from the Housatonic and Naugatuck valleys, and farmers' boys from the hills; of men of education and men of none. Though the large addition to its numbers which the increase in size necessitated made it perhaps somewhat less homogeneous than at first, it did not greatly alter its essential characteristics.

The records kept by the association referred to, furnish suggestive revelations as to the various elements that composed it. The names of men of every sort and kind are found upon the rolls. There were veterans of the Mexican War; there were refugees from the revolutionary uprisings in Europe of 1848; there were some who had served under compulsion in the armies of the South; there were men whose obviously fictitious names concealed stories which could be guessed to be extraordinary; there were names which have been for years among the best known and most honoured in this state; and there were those of outcasts and wrecks.

A large part of these men came back after their service ended to resume the peaceful life of citizenship, and every town among us has known some of them ever since among its leading figures, while some in quarters far distant have also attained to honours and responsibilities, as the records show. Connecticut has known for many years no small number of them as foremost in all lines of activity, and knows today, in official station and in private life, men of many honours, who count not least among these the fact that they were enrolled among the soldiers of the Second Connecticut Heavy Artillery.

MONUMENT AT ARLINGTON

The History of the
2nd Massachusetts
Regiment of Infantry

Daniel Oakey

Contents

A Paper Read at the Officers' Reunion in Boston,

May 12, 1884,

By

Daniel Oakey,

Captain Second Massachusetts

Regiment of Infantry.

Boston:

Beverly Ford

June 9, 1863.

In taking up the thread of Captain George A. Thayer's admirable chapter upon the Chancellorsville campaign, we find the regiment baling out their old log pens, on a dark night, in the rain. They had stripped the canvas roofs before starting for Chancellorsville. The return to a deserted camp, even in fine weather, flushed with victory, is not agreeable. The failure of Chancellorsville made the discomforts of this memorable night harder to bear, and it seemed very much like some of the worst experiences of the "Mud campaign."

Company "D" pursued their work with vigour, and sang with the broadest sarcasm "Home Again." This had rather an enlivening effect upon some of the other companies, who, up to this time, had been very silent. Daylight relieved us all; and, with sunshine and regimental "police," the place soon looked as if nothing had happened, except for the late absentees, some of whom would return when their wounds permitted; but others would never again draw their swords under the old battle-flag. The scholarly Fitzgerald, who died so bravely, was the only officer of "ours" killed at Chancellorsville.

It was at this very camp, about a month before, that the gallant and lamented Colonel Shaw, then a captain in our regiment, left us to organize and command that fated battalion, the "Fifty-fourth Coloured Massachusetts." Here, we again formed a mess with the officers of the Third Wisconsin; and our former caterer, Charley Johnson, and his coloured staff, managed the *table d'hôte*. Those who were fortunate enough to be present will remember the surprise party given to us by the officers of the Third Wisconsin in our canvas dining-room, at the foot of the hill, and how it burst upon us in all its splendour of bayonet chandeliers and unlimited "commissary." Brigade manoeuvres and battalion drills were diligently practised; and, when Casey's tactics were scarcely dry from the press, Colonel Sam Quincy, with the least possible preparation on our part, "sprung" on us the new movement of "Forward on the centre to form square" at "double-quick."

And, I am ashamed to say, that, practised as we were in all the tricks of field manoeuvres, we "got mixed." The right wing started without delay for Falmouth, the left wing for Acquia Creek, and the colour division took a steady trot for the camp of the Tenth Maine. Adjutant Fox galloped wildly about the field, the Colonel howled in despair, but on we went till the word "Halt!" brought us to a stand, and we came back and formed line. The Colonel then made the memorable remark, "Gentlemen will please to have some connection of ideas," and started the machine again at full speed. This time we melted into a square in a manner which would have pleased General Andrews. From this camp, Colonel Quincy resigned, pretty well exhausted with wounds, exposure, and the trials of the Rebel prison.

We now moved camp—Major Mudge commanding—to a pine grove, where we constructed quite a picturesque military village, and became absorbed in the habits and peculiarities of the wood-tick.

The days rolled on into June; and it seemed fully time to be doing something more about beating Lee, whose lieutenants were successfully screening their preparations for the coming Northern invasion. General Halleck, General-in-Chief at Washington, was still busily engaged telegraphing to the generals in the field; and, no doubt, Hooker was hampered by these voluminous instructions, often so at variance with his own plans, which were apt to be excellent, and he was unable at times to suppress his own dominant and rather insubordinate spirit.

On the 5th of June, Stuart was discovered concentrating his troopers in great force at Culpepper. Mr. Stuart's "Critter-back Company" was supposed to number about twelve thousand sabres, and information obtained by General Buford showed that the Rebels were preparing for a cavalry raid on a scale never before attempted.

Here was an opportunity for the "Cavalry Corps" which Hooker had organized; but, owing to the wear and tear of Stoneman's raid, General Hooker thought our cavalry weak to cope with the enemy, if their numbers as reported were correct. He decided, however, to send General Pleasanton with all the cavalry to attack Stuart, "stiffened," as he expressed it, with about five thousand infantry.

This "stiffening" consisted of a few selected regiments, including "ours," to be divided equally between two columns of cavalry,—one under Buford, with Ames to command his infantry, the other under Gregg, with General David Russell as infantry commander.

The total force of infantry was probably not more than three thousand, as each regiment was thinned down by weeding out every man who could not be relied upon for a forced march. The order came on the afternoon of June 6 to "get ready in light marching order for a secret expedition, leaving all sick and baggage behind." The news soon spread through camp, and friends from other regiments came to witness the departure of the chosen. Upon learning that the Third Wisconsin was not included in the order, the enthusiasm in the Second Massachusetts was considerably dampened.

"The Third" was certain that there must be some mistake in the transmission of the order. These two regiments had been brigaded together since the beginning of the war, and had fought side by side in every action. There was a sense of mutual support, and a desire to share equally all the honours; a strong feeling of pride in each regarding the achievements of the other. To us, it would have been unnatural to go into action without the Third Wisconsin, or at least not to know that they were in support. A hasty consultation resulted in sending an officer to present the case at head-quarters. The chaplain's excellent mare was summarily pressed for the service; and our ambassador, springing into the clerical saddle, shot away for General Ruger's head-quarters. He returned with an encouraging word that the General would see what could be done.

The column was already moving out of camp, under the gaze of a crowd of officers and men. It seemed quite a family affair, as we noticed the "Thirty-third Massachusetts" already on the road waiting for us, under the fatherly protection of Colonel Underwood, who had been so long a member of "ours" as captain of "the bloody I's."

Opinions were exchanged as to the probability of the Third Wisconsin getting its orders. Bets, of course, were freely offered and taken on the chances. Meantime, we were joined by a battery of horse artillery and a string of pack mules carrying extra ammunition. Presently, a battalion appeared coming over the hill at a pace indicating important business. Our cheering was taken up by the rest of the column; and the Third Wisconsin replied with wild howls, and quickly took their place as part of our special brigade.

After a furious thunder-shower, which laid the dust, General Ames gave the word; and the command moved off at a smart gait. The air was cool, and every member of the chosen band was in high spirits.

Even that army-trodden country, under the circumstances, and with the influence of a beautiful sunset, looked fresh and picturesque.

There was evidently a strong impression that we were able-bodied to the last man; for we skipped along for eight miles without a halt, in a style which impressed our cavalry friends, whom we found about eight o'clock in the evening drawn up in a field at the roadside, to give us the right of way. A voice came from one of the saddles, "I say, boys! what brigade?"

"Ah, you recruit!" replied one of the wits of the regiment: "don't you know this brigade? This is Gordon's flying brigade,"—which was received with much merriment. The men were in excellent humour, ready to bandy words with any one, especially the cavalry, whom they began to divine they were to operate with. This elegant repartee was kept up all along the line. Occasionally, officers exchanged greetings, where friends could make each other out in the dark. A hasty word and shake of the hand (perhaps the last), and our cavalry friend is left still watching the column as it marches briskly along.

Another cavalry detachment inquires: "What's your hurry, boys? Where are you going?"

"We're going to Richmond. Saddle up, you cowards, and come along!" A soldier in the next company, of an inquiring disposition, asks, "Who ever saw a dead cavalry man?"

We bivouacked near Spotted Tavern, about eleven o'clock at night; and, after this lively march of sixteen miles, we were allowed a comfortable rest, while the cavalry occupied the road.

Resuming our march at ten o'clock next day, we reached Bealton about sunset, and were carefully concealed in the woods. Lighting of fires was absolutely forbidden; and, as the night closed in upon us, the staff remained in the saddle, stationed at different points, silently watching us; and, as morning came again, there they were still on the watch.

Meantime, General Russell had marched his infantry to Hartwood Church, and thence to a point near Kelly's Ford, where General Gregg was concentrating two divisions of cavalry.

The night of the 8th, we moved down very near Beverly Ford into the woods again,—cold suppers and no lights. The men were exceedingly restless at these unusual orders about light and noise. In a letter from one of my men since the war, he says: "The men thought we were being humbugged, and there were many signs of dissatisfaction. They complained because we were not allowed to have fires.

Dave Orne was punished (ordered to stand at attention) by you, for snapping a cap upon his gun. It was exceedingly galling to his soldierly pride, as it was the only time he was punished during his term of service. Hyde was particularly insubordinate; and you were placed in arrest, because Company 'D' was so disorderly."

I remember this very well, and my servant standing at a respectful distance, holding my sabre while I was under this temporary cloud. The gallant commander of the "Irish Brigade," as we called Company "H," shared the cloud with me; for he was placed in arrest at the same time. Our sabres, however, were returned to us before we got into the fight; and, in the evening bivouac, our commander made us a most graceful apology over a tin mug of "commissary."

Buford's whole column was now concealed in the woods. The cheerful clank and jingle of the cavalry was, by some means, suppressed; there was no merry bugle breaking upon the still hours of the night; and, as the moon threw deep shadows across the quiet country road, there seemed no trace of "grim-visaged war."

At three o'clock in the morning, Captain Comey, with thirty picked men from the Second Massachusetts, crept down to the river-bank, to see that all was clear for the advance. He reported a large force of cavalry in bivouac on the south side of the river, quite unconscious of Buford's stealthy approach. Indeed, Jones' Rebel cavalry brigade was only a short distance from the Ford, while his wagons and artillery were parked even nearer to the river. Fitz Hugh Lee, Robertson, and W. H. F. Lee were in bivouac at various points within supporting distance of Jones; while Wade Hampton was passing the night in picturesque reserve at Fleetwood Hill.

The spot was admirably adapted for a cavalry battle, the country rolling along, with an occasional clump of woods and fine open fields, toward Brandy Station, where the Rebel cavalry-chief, Stuart, had pitched his head-quarters.

The close proximity of Stuart's troopers was a little unexpected. Their movement to Beverly Ford, it seems, was simultaneous with our own.

The plan was to have the enemy remain somewhere near Culpepper, while Gregg's column advanced from Kelly's Ford, and Buford's from Beverly Ford, the first bearing to the left, the latter to the right, the two columns to form a junction near Brandy Station. General Pleasanton then, having our entire force well in hand, would make a determined attack upon Stuart's squadrons. But it is the unexpected which must be looked for in war, and the necessary tactics were quickly decided upon.

Nearly the whole of Stuart's force was in our immediate front; but they would be exposed to the disadvantage of a surprise, and, having no infantry with them, our little brigade of rifles would be doubly effective.

General Pleasanton would be unable to control and harmonize the movements of his two columns, being completely cut off from General Gregg; but the latter was so well known as an able commander and a hard fighter that the enemy was certain to be treated again to a surprise in flank and rear, and would be thus diverted from our front. And it seemed as if we might still succeed in breaking up the enemy's cavalry.

The situation had its advantages, in spite of the opinion of some distinguished cavalry men; and "Forward!" was the word.

As the hazy June morning dawned upon us, troopers appeared to rise out of the ground and swarm out of the woods, till the whole country seemed alive with cavalry; and Ames' picked rifles took their place in the column.

The early morning mist, hanging upon the river banks, concealed our approach.

"In both our armies, there is many a soul Shall pay full dearly for this encounter, If once they join in trial."

The gallant and lamented Colonel Davis led the way with the Eighth New York Cavalry, dashing over the Ford and surprising the enemy's pickets, who fell back upon Jones' exposed artillery and wagons.

The Rebels were panic-stricken at the sudden approach of the "Yankee" cavalry; and great confusion ensued. But the alarm quickly spread, and part of Jones' troopers were soon in the saddle, charging furiously down upon the Eighth New York, who broke; and, before Colonel Davis could turn to rally his leading regiment, a Rebel soldier sprang from behind a tree and shot him dead. But the avenging sabre of Lieutenant Parsons (Davis' adjutant) severed the poor fellow's connection with this life.

Colonel Davis was a serious loss to the "Cavalry Corps,"—a graduate of West Point, an accomplished officer, a universal favourite,—and, although a Southerner, he stuck to the flag he had sworn to defend.

Meantime, the Eighth Illinois Cavalry had gained the southern bank, and rushed upon Jones' people, driving them back upon the main body, who were forming in the rear of a bit of wood. Colonel Davis was borne back in a blanket as General Pleasanton, who had accompanied our column in person, arrived at the river bank.

The Third Indiana Cavalry followed the Eighth Illinois; and Ames' men were now crossing under the eye of the distinguished group of horsemen, to one of whom (Colonel F. C. Newhall, afterward of Sheridan's staff) I am indebted for the following description:—

General Buford was there, with his usual smile. He rode a gray horse, at a slow walk generally, and smoked a pipe, no matter what was going on around him; and it was always reassuring to see him in the saddle when there was any chance of a fight.

General Pleasanton's staff was partly composed of men who became distinguished. The Adjutant General was A. J. Alexander, of Kentucky, a very handsome fellow, who was afterward a Brigadier General with Thomas, in the West. Among the *aides* was Captain Farnsworth, Eighth Illinois Cavalry, who so distinguished himself in the coming battle, and in the subsequent operations south of the Potomac, that he was made a Brigadier General, and with that rank fell at Gettysburg, at the head of a brigade of cavalry which he had commanded but a few days. Another *aide* was the brilliant Custer, then a lieutenant, whose career and lamented death there is no need to recall.

Another was Lieutenant R. S. McKenzie, of the engineers, now General McKenzie of well-won fame, the youngest colonel of the regular army; and still another was Ulric Dahlgren. General Pleasanton had certainly no lack of intelligence, dash, and hard-riding to rely on in those about him.

The infantry had now cleared the woods of the enemy's troopers, who were deceived as to the number of our rifles, and showed no inclination to expose men and horses to the deadly fire of experienced infantry skirmishers.

The old, time-honoured Second Dragoons, the Fifth Regulars, and that crack young regiment, the Sixth Pennsylvania Cavalry (forming what was known as the "Reserve Brigade"), were massing on the southern bank of the river. The sharp report of infantry rifles, the rising smoke, and the thousand indescribable sounds, with the tramp of fresh cavalry pressing forward to take their part in the fray, showed that the battle was now waging in good earnest. The wounded arrived more rapidly at the ford, stretcher-bearers plying their trade in the hot sun.

The soft, dewy grass of the morning was now kicked and trampled into dry dust. The infantry held the enemy in the open space beyond the woods; while Buford hurled his squadrons, with drawn sabres, upon the Rebel cavalry on the right and left.

A sabre charge, with both sides going at top speed, is, perhaps, the most exciting and picturesque combination of force, nerve, and courage that can be imagined. The commanding officers leading in conspicuous advance; the rush, the thunder of horses' hoofs; the rattle of arms and equipments,—all mingling with the roar of voices, while the space rapidly lessens between the approaching squadrons. The commanders who were seen, a moment before, splendidly mounted, dashing on at racing speed, turning in the saddle to look back at the tidal wave which they are leading, disappear in a cloud of sabres, clashing and cutting; but the fight is partly obscured by the rising dust and the mist from the over-heated animals.

Riderless horses come, wounded and trembling, out of the melee; others appear, running in fright, carrying dying troopers still sitting their chargers, the head drooping on the breast, the sword-arm hanging lifeless, the blood-stained sabre dangling from the wrist, tossing, swinging, and cutting the poor animal's flanks, goading him on in his aimless flight. In this moment of intense excitement, the Rebels give way on the left. Our troopers follow in hot pursuit. On they go, over the dead and dying. At the sound of the "recall," back they come, to take breath and re-form at the rallying ground to which Ames' skirmishers move forward, to regain their connection and establish a more advanced line of battle.

Although the infantry occupied the centre of the line, their operations were not confined to this point. They were sent in small detachments to different parts of the field, to support artillery, and, at times, even to engage the enemy, when opportunity offered. The line officers bore a thorough test of their experience and training during a day of perpetual activity.

The "Reserve Brigade" had gone into action. There were to be no fresh troops in waiting. Everyone was needed at the front.

The Rebels made desperate attempts to capture the ford, and pressed us hard on the right. This part of our line made little progress, and was forced at times to assume simply the defensive.

Two squadrons of the Second Dragoons were withdrawn to assist in covering the approaches to the ford.

The Rebels made another desperate charge. It seemed, this time, as if they would carry all before them. But we stood our ground, and opened on them at close quarters with the guns; and Ames' men plied their rifles, making every bullet tell. The enemy lost heavily, and came to a stand. The Dragoons dropped their carbines, and, drawing sabres, rushed upon them, driving them off in confusion.

It was hot work all along the line; and, although our cavalry suffered severely at times, nothing could surpass their gallant conduct.

The Sixth Pennsylvania, in charging the enemy near St. James' Church, were badly punished by the Rebel artillery, and had to withdraw with heavy loss of officers, men, and horses. Their gallant commander, Major Morris, whose horse fell upon him, was left a prisoner in the enemy's hands. The Second Dragoons also suffered severely at this point.

Much to our relief, the enemy now appeared to be attacked in the rear, as they made no further attempt to capture the ford, and the force in our front was evidently reduced.

A Rebel battery now opened from a bit of woods about six hundred yards in front, while we were making disposition to advance our right, and our guns unlimbered upon a knoll in the open fields in front and to the right of the ford; and a lively cannonade ensued. I was skirmishing nearer to the centre of the line with my own company and Company "F," the latter under command of Captain, then Lieutenant, Parker, and was ordered with these two companies to support the guns on the knoll.

On the way, I was joined by Colonel, then Captain, Stevenson of the Third Wisconsin, who had been ordered to the same duty. General Buford and some staff officers were standing near the guns, their horses awaiting them in the rear, where the artillery horses had taken refuge.

Part of the Tenth Virginia Cavalry were on foot behind a stone wall down in the open fields in front; and they endeavoured to interfere with us as much as possible while we were posting Lieutenant Parker with two men as a "lookout" to apprise us of any movement on the part of the enemy. They had already annoyed our artillery very much, popping at them with their carbines.

Captain Stevenson and I lay down with our companies in the usual position of artillery supports, about thirty yards in rear, while our guns belched forth their fire and smoke, and the enemy's shells came howling overhead and bursting behind us with that spiteful, sharp, clean-cut bang which we used to know so well.

Having nothing to do as yet but smoke our pipes, we lolled on the grass and studied our cavalry friends. Custer was the most striking figure in the group, with his fanciful uniform, his long hair, and spirited manner. He seemed to enjoy the shelling, and appeared to beam all over, almost dancing with excitement.

Other staff officers arrived from time to time, and, plunging into the group, on their reeking horses, spoke to General Buford, and then dashed away again. The fight seemed still going on in the centre and on the left, which had advanced considerably; but our view was somewhat obstructed by clumps of woods.

General Buford, whom we had never seen before, impressed us with his commanding presence and his manly and picturesque simplicity of dress. He looked as if his division might idolize him, as it was said they did. He seemed much annoyed at the Tenth Virginia Cavalry behind the wall, and at last summoned the commander of the infantry supports. Although Stevenson commanded, he wished me to assist at the audience; and we were at the General's side in a moment, looking over the guns at the surrounding country.

"Do you see those people down there?" says Buford: "they've got to be driven out. Do you think you can do it?"

We looked up and down the line, and rested our gaze upon a wheat-field on the left of the stone wall (the enemy's right).

"It's about double our force," says Stevenson.

"Fully that," I replied, "if not more."

We looked again at the wheat-field, for that was the key to the position. Something was said about "flanking" and "enfilading 'em."

"Mind," said the General, "I don't order you; but, if you think you can do it, go in."

We thought we could. It would hardly do to back out in the presence of so distinguished a cavalry audience, if there was a chance of success. A number of the staff had gathered round to hear our conversation, and showed a great deal of interest at the prospect of a little "side show," at which they would have orchestra chairs, front row.

The General, with this group around him, was drawing the fire of the stone wall people, and was urged to keep out of range, while the rest of us scattered to less dangerous positions. Some of the staff came back and watched the men "fall in," as if to see us off. Custer showed much interest, and evidently would have enjoyed going with us.

We struck back into the country, and took a circuitous route behind hedges and through corn-fields, Stevenson and myself running on together, and the men following with their rifles as low as possible, and crouching along to avoid attracting any notice.

We planned the attack as we went along, instructing sergeants, who in turn fell back and gave orders to the men. Upon arriving at the wheat-field, we all hugged the ground. Ten picked marksmen now crawled forward with me into the wheat, while Captain Stevenson deployed the rest of the men into as long a skirmish line as their numbers would permit.

We despatched a messenger to notify Lieutenant Parker, whom we had left near the guns, to join us at once. In justice to Parker, I must say that he hated to be left out of a fight.

The ten marksmen crawled on through the wheat, till they were almost "on the end" of the enemy's line; and then, crowding together so as to rake the line, they fired at the signal, with terrible accuracy.

The Rebels were completely surprised, but turned and delivered a scattering fire. My excellent Sergeant Nutting fell into my arms mortally wounded. He was all pluck to the last moment. Although he could not speak, he showed signs of wishing to bid us good-by, and was evidently gratified at the manner in which we tenderly shook him by the hand. It was a success for the company, but the men all seemed to share my own feeling that it was dearly bought at such a price.

Meantime, Captain Stevenson was advancing through the wheat; and, as soon as my party fired, he began making noise enough for two regiments. We sprang over the fence into the open field; and there we found Lieutenant Parker standing on the stone wall, pistol in hand, with his two men and the messenger, demanding "unconditional surrender."

We could not help being amused at Parker's sudden appearance; but he explained that he was afraid that he would be too late, and so "charged the stone wall in front, and took the chances."

Stevenson's men were coming over the fence all the way down the wheat; and the enemy, utterly deceived as to our numbers, had already commenced dropping their weapons and giving themselves up. We hurried them off as rapidly as possible, and gave all the care we could to the wounded. Some of the Rebels at the other end of the wall tried to escape; but Stevenson had swung his line round so promptly that he covered them at short range, and persuaded the runaways to come in.

Having killed, wounded, and captured the entire party, we retired to a rising ground to the left of our own guns, and covered the approaches to the stone wall by posting some sharp-shooters with their pieces sighted at three hundred yards. At this distance, two of the enemy's dismounted troopers were killed. This seemed to be sufficient warning to the rest, who made no further attempt to occupy the stone wall.

General Buford now advanced the right of the line, and pressed forward, driving the enemy's cavalry before him toward Fleetwood Hill. General Gregg, who had relieved us at such a critical moment by diverting the enemy from our front, had crossed Kelly's Ford at daylight with little opposition, and left General Russell with his infantry to guard the lower fords.

Colonel Duffie's division was sent to Stevensburg, where they encountered the enemy, and drove them through and beyond the town, with our friends of the First Massachusetts Cavalry in the advance; and here Colonel Duffie remained, according to the original plan.

General Gregg pushed on toward Brandy Station with Kilpatrick's and Windham's brigades. The latter attacked the Rebel cavalry so promptly that they were scarcely ready for him. Stuart's head-quarters were captured and important despatches fell into our hands, with valuable information as to the enemy's plans. Windham and Kilpatrick were both hotly engaged as troops were withdrawn from Buford's front to resist them.

Gregg's people fought hard, charging repeatedly with the sabre, and gradually gaining the crest of Fleetwood Hill. The Sixth New York Light Battery did their full share of work.

More troops were withdrawn from Buford's front; and, at last, General Gregg, finding himself overmatched, withdrew to the foot of the hill, leaving two guns in the enemy's hands. Colonel H. S. Thomas describes the cannoneers reluctantly obeying the order to leave the guns, some of the men actually shedding tears.

Meanwhile, General Buford continued to push the enemy toward Fleetwood, and again the Rebels began to resist us more stubbornly. Both sides charged repeatedly with the sabre, and at times dismounted to fight behind stone walls, Ames' rifles making themselves generally useful at various points in the field.

In one very spirited charge of the Second Dragoons, General Merritt, then a captain, rode impetuously on, not hearing the recall, followed by Lieutenant Quirk. He noticed a prominent Rebel officer, and, riding toward him, bringing his sabre to a point, he innocently remarked, "Colonel, you are my prisoner!"

The officer made a cut at his head: Merritt, dexterously parrying the cut, only lost his hat. His opponent turned out to be Colonel, afterward, General Wade Hampton. Lieutenant Quirk called out to Merritt, "We're surrounded!" and, sure enough, a Rebel ring had formed to see the "Yankee" officer brought down. But Merritt and Quirk had not been taught to ride for nothing, and galloped safely back into our lines, amid a shower of pistol bullets.

General Rodenbough, then a captain, and many others of the cavalry, had personal encounters, in which they proved themselves to be excellent swordsmen.

As our two columns drew nearer together, both aiming for Fleetwood Hill, the junction was at last accomplished; and General Gregg rode into our lines, reporting a heavy force of Rebel infantry pouring into Brandy Station from Culpepper by rail.

General Pleasanton not caring to encounter the Rebel infantry, especially after a day of such hard pounding, ordered General Gregg to withdraw by way of Rappahannock Station; and Colonel Newhall was sent to tell Buford to stop fighting, and go home by way of Beverly Ford.

The operation of withdrawal was accomplished without interference, the enemy contenting themselves with looking on from a respectful distance. As we approached Beverly Ford, the First Regular Cavalry turned up, eager for the fray. They had been off on some detached duty and were too late for any of the fun, so General Pleasanton had them all deployed as mounted skirmishers to cover the crossing of the troops.

The scene at the ford was very picturesque. A lovely sunset shed its cool light over the long columns of cavalry winding their way toward the river, and the mounted skirmishers were thrown in bold relief against the brilliant sky.

Captain Comey took his old position again, with his little band of thirty men, on the north bank of the river, and remained there till morning, when he rejoined the regiment.

Our bivouac the night of the battle was unusually cheerful, for we had brought every officer of "ours" safely out of the fight alive and well. Even Captain Frank Crowninshield, who generally got a bullet into him somewhere, came off, like the Irishman at the fair, with only a hole in the crown of his hat.

Many a fence rail was burned to give light to the conference which was held over the events of the day. We had been so separated during the fight that the experiences of each one had to be presented to the assemblage in turn; and, with the assistance of some of the Third Wisconsin officers, the comparing of notes was extended far into the night.

Our forces had gained all they set out to accomplish. The momentous cavalry schemes of the enemy were frustrated, and their troopers had been severely punished by cavalry which they had always considered inferior to their own.

The disheartening effect throughout the Confederacy may be guessed by the following extract from a diary kept by Mr. I. D. Jones, the Rebel War Clerk at Richmond:—

June 12.—The surprise of Stuart on the Rappahannock has chilled every heart, notwithstanding it does not appear that we lost more than the enemy in the encounter. The question is on every tongue, Have our generals relaxed in vigilance? If so, sad is the prospect.

After the long period of mismanagement, disaster, sacrifice, blood, and tears through which the Army of the Potomac had passed, with steadiness of purpose and undaunted courage which has never been surpassed, the turning-point came, at last, in the brilliant conflict at Beverly Ford, or "Fleetwood," as the Rebel chief, Stuart, called it.

It was a severe blow to the enemy's cavalry at the right moment, and was productive of important results, being followed by Pleasanton in the battles of Aldie, Middleburg, and Upperville, holding Stuart in check and keeping Hooker fully informed as to the movements of the enemy; while General Lee was in constant anxiety and in want of information during his march up the Cumberland Valley and, in fact, during the whole of the Gettysburg campaign. On the 27th of June, General Hooker requested to be relieved, and General Mead assumed command of the Army of the Potomac.

This change of commanders was accomplished while the two great armies were in motion. There was no excitement over it. The Army of the Potomac was not very sorry to part with General Hooker, nor specially pleased to be commanded by Mead. On the whole, they had more confidence in the latter; but the main object was to beat Lee.

Frontier Service During the Rebellion

George H. Pettis

Contents

Frontier Service During
the Rebellion

The first battle of Bull Run had been fought. The government had become satisfied that the slaveholder's rebellion was not to be put down with seventy-five thousand men. The Union people of the United States now fully realized that the rebels were to use every effort on their part towards the establishment of the Confederacy, and the men of the north, on their part, were ready to "mutually pledge to each other our lives, our fortunes, and our sacred honour" to preserve the government as their fathers before them had pledged themselves to establish it. The loyal States were ready to respond to any demand made upon them by the government, and there were none more anxious to do their duty to the old flag than the Union men of California.

The people of that far distant part of our country were, in the early days of our "late unpleasantness," stirred to their very depths. A large portion of the inhabitants had emigrated from the southern States, and were, therefore, in sympathy with their brethren at home. General Albert Sidney Johnston was in command of the military department, and a majority of the regular officers under him were sympathizers with the rebellion, as were a majority of the State officers. The United States gunboat *Wyoming*, lying in the harbour of San Francisco in the early part of '61, was officered by open advocates of secession, and only by the secret coming of General E.V. Sumner, who arrived by steamer one fine morning in the early part of '61, totally unknown and unannounced, and presenting himself at the army headquarters on Washington street, San Francisco, without delay, with, "Is this General Johnston?"

"Yes, sir."

"I am General E. V. Sumner, United States Army, and do now relieve you of the command of this department," at the same time delivering the orders to this effect from the War Department at Washington, were the people of the Pacific States saved from a contest which would have been more bitter, more fierce, and more unrelenting than was exhibited in any part of the United States during all those long four years of the war.

As I have said before, the prompt and secret action of the government and that gallant old soldier, General E. V. Sumner (for you all will remember that California had no railroads and telegraphs in those days), prevented civil war there. The secessionists, who were preparing to take possession of the property of the government in that department and turn the guns of Alcatraz, Fort Point and the Presidio upon the loyalists, were taken completely aback; they delayed action.

General Sumner took all precautions against surprise, and the Union men of the Pacific States breathed free again, for civil war had been driven from their doors. Many of the secession leaders, with General Albert Sidney Johnston, seeing their plans miscarry, left the State shortly after, and did service in the Confederate armies.

On the steamer from the States that brought the news to California of the disaster at Bull Run, came orders from President Lincoln for that State to furnish its quota of men for the Union army. The same afternoon, the Franklin Light Infantry, a militia company, composed of printers only, held a meeting at its armoury on Sacramento street, and voted unanimously to offer their services to the government, which was accordingly done, and they were the first company that was mustered into the United States service in California, and was afterwards known as Company B, First Infantry, California Volunteers, and were officered as follows: Captain, Valentine Drescher; First Lieutenant, Francis S. Mitchell; Second Lieutenant, George H. Pettis. Other companies were soon formed, and the regiment, with nine companies, went into camp of instruction at Camp Downey, near Oakland.

The regiment had been in camp but a few days when it was ordered to proceed by steamer to Los Angeles, in Southern California. The transfer was made, and the regiment went into camp about nine miles from Los Angeles, on the seashore, where the town of Santa Monica now is. The First Battalion Cavalry, California Volunteers, consisting of five companies, under command of Lieutenant Colonel Davis, who was afterwards killed before Richmond, also accompanied us. In a few days after the establishment of this camp, Lieutenant Pettis, of Company B, was sent on detached duty as recruiting officer to San Francisco, in order that the nine companies now in camp should be filled to the maximum standard. The tenth company had not been admitted to the regiment as yet, although several had made application for the position.

Lieutenant Pettis arrived in San Francisco about the fifteenth of October, and immediately commenced business by opening his recruiting office on the corner of Montgomery and Clay streets, in the same building with the *Morning Call*. He was successful, as by the fifteenth of January he had recruited and sent to the regiment one hundred and two men, and was ordered by General George Wright, then commanding the department of California (and who was afterwards lost on the steamer *Brother Jonathan* on his way to Oregon), to close his office and join his regiment at Camp Latham. In the meantime, four companies of the regiment, under Major E. A. Rigg, had proceeded to Fort Yuma, on the Colorado River, and relieved the regulars who were there. Captain Winfield Scott Hancock, Assistant Quartermaster United States Army, had also been relieved and ordered to the States. He had been on duty at Los Angeles.

Three companies of the regiment had been ordered to Warner's Ranch, about half way between Los Angeles and Fort Yuma, and established Camp Wright. On the twelfth of February, orders had been received by Colonel J. H. Carleton, commanding the regiment, to form the tenth company of his regiment from the recruits enlisted in San Francisco by Lieutenant Pettis. Company K, First Infantry, California Volunteers, was thus formed, and was officered as follows: Captain, Nicholas S. Davis, promoted from First Lieutenant of Company A; First Lieutenant, George H. Pettis, promoted from Second Lieutenant of Company B; Second Lieutenant, Jeremiah Phelan, appointed from Hospital Steward of the regular army.

In the meantime, the government at Washington had received information that General H. H. Sibley had left San Antonio, Texas, with about three thousand seven hundred rebel soldiers for New Mexico, and as the government had immense stores of clothing, camp and garrison equipage, and commissary stores in different posts in that Territory and Arizona, with but few troops to defend them, and a majority of the officers avowed secessionists, the rebels expected an easy conquest. Accordingly, Colonel Carleton had orders to organize what was known as the "California Column," which consisted of the First and Fifth Infantry, California Volunteers, (George W. Bowie was Colonel of the Fifth Infantry, California Volunteers); First Battalion Cavalry, California Volunteers; Company B, Captain John C. Cremoney, Second Cavalry, California Volunteers, and Light Battery A, Third United States Artillery, Captain John B. Shinn.

That an idea may be obtained of the difficulties of this enterprise, I will say that it is about nine hundred miles from Los Angeles to the Rio Grande, not a pound of food or of forage was to be obtained on the route, and everything to be consumed had to be brought from California. Neither was there, as we afterwards ascertained, a single resident in all that long march, except at Fort Yuma. The country through which the "Column" passed was without water, and the Colorado and Gila Deserts to be crossed before we should come in sight of the green cottonwoods of the Rio Grande.

The Apache Indians supposed that they had driven all the whites out of the Territory of Arizona, and the former required constant watching and attention. In consequence of the scarcity of water on the route, the "Column" could only be moved in detachments.

Companies K and C, First Infantry, and Company G, Fifth Infantry, Captain Hugh L. Hinds, left Captain Latham about the first of March, 1862, under command of Captain William McMullen, of Company C, and arrived at Camp Wright in due season, it being about one hundred and forty miles. The only incident on this march worthy of mention was, that when the battalion marched through the town of Los Angeles the American flag had been hauled down from the court house. As it was well known that the people of Los Angeles at that time were nearly all strong in their sympathies with the rebellion, it was thought that the hauling down of the flag was to insult the command.

Consequently, on the arrival of the battalion on the banks of the Los Angeles river, which flows on the eastern side of the town, it was halted and Captain McMullen returned, and, finding some of the town officials, insisted that the flag should be hoisted immediately. The citizens denied any intended insult to the flag, and proceeded to replace it, which being seen by the men of the battalion, they gave three cheers, and continued on their way.

A delay of a couple of weeks at Camp Wright, when orders were received by Lieutenant Colonel J. R. West, of the First Infantry, commanding at Camp Wright, to organize the advance detachment of the "Column," to consist of Companies K and C, First Infantry, California Volunteers, and Companies B and G, Fifth Infantry, California Volunteers, and proceed without delay to Fort Yuma. The command as above constituted left camp at a late hour in the afternoon, and after a short march made camp beside a *laguna*, or pond. It rained during the night, and daylight found us at breakfast, which was quickly dispatched, and we were soon on our march, the road continually ascending.

At nine o'clock in the forenoon we had reached the line of snow, where it was snowing heavily. At noon we had reached the summit, and found the snow about two feet in depth, and as cold as Greenland. A short halt was made, when great fires were built to warm the men, and then the command moved down the mountain. At three o'clock in the afternoon we passed through the line of snow, shortly after through the precipitous canon of San Felipe, and towards evening went into camp, the grass being more than knee high, the air redolent with the perfume of flowers and the sweet melody of the birds.

A short march the next day brought us to Los Dos Palmas, or the "Two Palms," so called from the fact that two luxuriant palm trees formerly flourished here, the stumps of which were then to be seen. Thence to Carizo Creek, nine miles, where the command rested one day. Here commences the then much-dreaded Colorado Desert. For more than a hundred miles we were at the mercy of its sands and storms and burning sun. Such another scene of desolation does not exist on the American continent; treeless mountains on either side, brown and sombre to their very tops; no signs of life were to be seen anywhere. Although it was in the first days of April, still the sun poured down with an intensity that I had never before experienced, no shade could be found, and the very water in the creek could not be bathed in—being more fit for cooking than bathing, it being so hot. Such was the Colorado Desert as we approached it. What will it be further on? We shall see.

The command left camp at Carizo Creek in the middle of the afternoon, and continued the march until midnight, when we arrived at Sackett's Wells. Here it was supposed a ration of water for the men would be found, but upon examination it was ascertained that somebody had knocked the bottom out of the well, and no water was to be obtained, except such as could be caught in cups as it trickled drop by drop from the strata of clay that had heretofore formed the bottom of the well.

No camp could be made here, and the command moved on, marching until about ten o'clock in the morning, when we arrived at the Indian Wells, having made thirty-two miles. A large number of the men were now suffering for the want of water, and the animals, upon discovering the green bushes in the distance, near these wells, pricked their ears, and every exertion was required by riders and drivers to prevent a stampede, so much were they in want of water.

Upon our arrival it was found that but a few buckets of water was in the well, as a detachment of cavalry had made camp there the day before, and had only left upon seeing our command approach, using all the water in the well for their animals before leaving. However, guards were placed over the well, men sent down to pass the water up as it collected, and in the course of a few hours the men had each received his pint of water; then the animals were furnished.

Before the water had all been distributed, one of those terrible sand storms for which this desert is renowned began, and as the sun went down it was at its very height. Neither man nor animal could face this shower of stones and gravel, and the sand and dust penetrated everything. The only thing that was to be done was to throw oneself down upon his face, draw his blankets around him, and ride it out, sleeping. The storm continued through the night, and before dawn approached it had ceased, and upon crawling out of my sand bank, I saw in all directions what appeared to be graves, but they were only mounds of sand that had been formed by the storm over the bodies of the soldiers. Imagine, if you can, near four hundred of these mounds becoming animate and dissolving in the desert, as reveille sounded.

At about noon the command moved on, and after marching twenty-five miles arrived at Alamo Mucho at about two o'clock in the morning. Here was found a well that would have furnished water for an army corps—sweet, cold water. It was a pleasure to look at this, to hold it in a tin cup, look at it, take a mouthful, holding it there a time before swallowing it; it seemed a sin to drink it. This water was not taken on the point of the bayonet, as water had been taken for the past four days, and we had marched sixty-six miles from Los Dos Palmos since we had our fill of water.

After the men had satisfied their thirst they spread their blankets wherever they pleased, and there was no person in that command, except the guard, that was not soon in the arms of Morpheus.

Before daylight another sand storm commenced, and when reveille was beat off, not a dozen men were in line, and they were only brought out of their sand hills by beating the long roll. The storm subsided in the early afternoon, when the command moved on, making Gardiner's Wells, twelve miles, before sundown, where was found a fine well with plenty of water, but none of the command wanted any, the only objection being, and that a slight one, that there was standing above the level of the water in the well, a pair of boots—and a dead man in them.

Seven Wells was soon reached, and, as the name implies, there were plenty of wells, but there was no water. Thence to Cook's Well, twelve miles, with plenty of good water, thence fourteen miles to the Colorado river, at Algodones. The next day, before noon, the command arrived at Fort Yuma and went into camp. Here we met Don Pascual, a head chief of the Yumas, Don Diego Jaeger, and the "Great Western," three of the most celebrated characters in the annals of Fort Yuma.

It was supposed that our command was to constitute the advance of the "Column" from Fort Yuma. But upon our arrival at that point, we found that a reconnoitering party, consisting of Company I, First California Infantry, Captain W. P. Calloway; Company A, First California Cavalry, Captain William McLeave, and Lieutenant Phelan, with detachments for two mountain howitzers, had been sent up the Gila River, as the Indians had reported that a large body of rebels were advancing on Fort Yuma from Tucson.

On the third day after our arrival we crossed over the Colorado River and continued our march. We passed the divide between the Colorado and Gila Rivers, and arrived at Gila City that afternoon, eighteen miles. Our route was the old overland stage route on the south side of the Gila. Here we first saw that peculiar and picturesque cactus, so characteristic of the country, called by the Indians *petayah*, but more generally known as the *suaro*, and recognized by botanists as the *Cereus grandeus*.

Our next march was to Filibuster camp, eleven miles; thence to Antelope Peak, fifteen; Mohawk, twelve; Texas Hill, eleven; Stanwix, seventeen; Burke's, twelve miles. Here we found the reconnoitering party, under Captain Calloway, that had left Fort Yuma a few days before our arrival there. They had had a brush with the rebels at Picacho, a point about forty-five miles west of Tucson. Lieutenant Barrett, Company A, First Cavalry, California Volunteers, and three men of the same company, had been killed. They had secured three rebel prisoners. The poor devils were under guard beneath some cottonwoods in their camp. They were now on their return to Fort Yuma.

The next morning our command moved out with more alacrity than usual, for we felt that we were now the advance of the "Column," and we would meet the rebels, too. A short march of twelve miles brought us to Oatman Flat. We had come down from the high mesa lands into this valley, and as we passed through near the middle of it, saw upon the right side of the road a small enclosure of rails, on one end of which was inscribed "The Oatman Family."

We had all heard of this tragedy years before, and now we were upon the spot where the terrible massacre had been perpetrated. No one of us could look upon this humble monument without awakening a feeling of revenge, and many were the silent pledges given that day that when the opportunity should offer, that at least one shot would be given for these silent victims to Indian treachery. One officer was so affected that he approached Colonel J. R. West, our commanding officer, with the interrogatory: "Colonel, if we should at anytime meet any of these Indians, what course should be pursued towards them?"

"Tell your men when they see a head, hit it if they can!" was the colonel's quick rejoinder. You may think this to have been rather harsh, but remember we were standing above the remains of the innocent victims of a most terrible tragedy.

A few miles after leaving Oatman's Flat we came to a pile of immense boulders in the centre of a pleasant valley. These were the famous "*Pedras Pintados*," or painted rocks. A march of fourteen miles brought the command to Kenyon's. The next day, after sixteen miles marching, we arrived at Gila Bend. Here we lay over a day, as our next march was to be to the Maricopa Wells, forty miles distant, the dreaded Gila Desert.

After marching all night and all of the next day, we approached the Maricopa Wells at about twelve o'clock on the second night. When within a mile of this point, a small reconnoitering party that had been sent ahead of our command, met us and reported that a large force of the rebels had possession of the wells, and from appearances intended to prevent our command from reaching there. This report served to put new life into everybody, notwithstanding that the whole command had now been without sleep for over forty hours, had marched forty miles and was somewhat fatigued.

One company was thrown out as skirmishers, the rest of the command in line of battle. We approached the watering place, and when we arrived there, instead of finding a formidable enemy, we found a half a dozen of our own cavalry that had been scouting ahead of the command. We found the water strongly impregnated with alkali, but it served to assuage our thirst.

A short march of ten miles then brought us to the Casa Blanca, the largest village of the Pimo Indians. Our command remained here for several weeks, until at least a large part of the "Column" had arrived, and large stores of commissaries and forage had been collected. Our Indian scouts and spies brought every few days extravagant reports of the force of rebels at Tucson, and they all agreed that when our troops should reach that point, we would meet with a warm reception, and that rifle-pits, sufficiently manned, extended a long ways on either side of the town.

These Indians were on the best of terms with us, as they had sold large amounts of their produce to our command, for which they had been promptly and abundantly paid—a different experience when the rebels were there. They had been employed by our quartermaster's department as herders of our beef cattle, and were paid to their own satisfaction for all services they had rendered, but no inducement that our commander offered them, no amount of pay, could influence any one of them to accompany us towards Tucson, so assured were they that we were to be "wiped out" before we should reach there.

On or about the twelfth day of May, 1862, the advance, constituted as before stated, with B Company, California Cavalry, Captain Emil Fritz, added, left the peaceful and hospitable homes of the Pimos, and arrived at the Sacatone, twelve miles. Here we left the overland mail road, which we had followed since leaving Los Angeles, and keeping up the south bank of the Gila to White's Ranch; thence to the celebrated ruins of the Casa Blanca, so graphically described by Mr. John R. Bartlett in his *Personal Narratives* of the Boundary Commission; thence to Rattlesnake Spring; thence to old Fort Breckenridge, which had been so cowardly deserted the year before by our regular troops; thence to Canon de Oro.

As we now approached Tucson, everything was in fighting trim. A short halt was made near the town, and the cavalry company, in two divisions, approached the place from the north and west. The infantry marched in by the main street from the west, with the field music playing "Yankee Doodle," and instead of being received by shot and shell, we found neither friend nor enemy, only a village without population, if we except some hundreds of dogs and cats.

When we were at the Pimos, Governor Pesquira, of Sonora, Mexico, arrived there from California on his way home; he was allowed to pass our lines; he and his party arrived in Tucson a few days before our command, and found the place nearly deserted. Captain Hunter, with his rebel soldiers, were far on their way to the Rio Grande, and as they had assured the native population—wholly Mexican—that when the "Abs"—meaning the Union troops—arrived they would massacre all the men and abuse all the women, they stood not upon the order of going, but went at once for Sonora.

Governor Pesquira hurried forward, overtaking parties of the fugitives each day, and assuring them of different treatment from the Union soldiers than they had been told by the rebels, induced many to return to their homes, and within a week Tucson was again alive; stores and gambling saloons were numerous, the military had taken possession of the best buildings in the town for quarters, and the stars and stripes again waved over the Capital of the Territory of Arizona.

The advance of the "Column" entered Tucson on the twentieth day of May, 1862. Several Americans, among them Sylvester Mowry, formerly of Rhode Island, returned, and being violent in their sympathies with the rebellion, were arrested. Some were sent out of the Territory, while Mowry was sent to Fort Yuma, where he remained incarcerated a long time. About the fifteenth of June, Captain N. S. Davis was relieved from the command of Company K by Lieutenant Pettis, who remained in command, with a short interval, until its final muster out. Captain Davis was on duty in the quartermaster's department.

By the first of July, a large part of the "Column" had arrived at Tucson, a large depot of army stores had been brought from California, and preparations were commenced for the movement again of the advance column. Several spies and scouts had been sent forward from Tucson, but as they had not returned, matters were rather uncertain. However, in the first week in July, Company E, First California Infantry, Captain Thomas L. Roberts, and Company B, Second California Cavalry, were ordered to proceed to Apache Pass and hold possession of the water at that point.

On the twentieth of July the advance column left Tucson, and on the second day arrived at the San Pedro, twenty-five miles. Here a delay of one day was made to put the fording place in good order for the crossing of the "Column." Information was received here that Captain Roberts' advance into the Apache Pass had been attacked by a large force of the Apaches, under the renowned chief, "Cochise," and after fighting during an entire afternoon had succeeded in driving the Indians, with a loss on our side of several of our men killed and wounded.

Our next march was to Dragoon Springs, eighteen miles; thence

100

to Sulphur Springs, twenty-two miles. The famous Apache Pass was reached by another march of twenty-five miles. Here was found the command of Captain Roberts, with evidences of the struggle of a few days before. On leaving Apache Pass the next day, we were again the advance of the "Column," which position was retained until our arrival on the Rio Grande.

The next camping ground was at San Simon, eighteen miles. As we were assured by our guides that no water would be found until we reached *Ojo de Vaca*, or Cow Springs, a distance of sixty-seven miles, it was deemed advisable to leave the overland route at this point, and proceed by another route. Accordingly, the next morning the command moved south, following up the San Simon Valley, a distance of twelve miles, and camped at the Cienega. Here was found water, the best and most abundant on the whole march. Imagine, if you can, a valley twenty miles in width, on either side a range of mountains; and to the north and south, up and down the valley, a level plain as far as the eye could reach.

A trench three feet wide, by five or six in depth, filled nearly to the top with clear cold water, running with a velocity of at least six miles an hour, the bottom covered with white smooth pebbles. Two miles above this point no water was to be found. As you descended the valley and approached this water, you found at first the ground moist, then water appeared, a mere drop, then a small stream of running water, which increased in volume, until you found a stream as described above.

Below this point the water gradually lessened, until, two miles below, this magnificent stream had entirely disappeared. There was no shade to be had here, except that found under the wagon bodies, still there was no fault found; the fine stream of water that we were enjoying satisfied us for all other discomforts. It was with feelings of regret that we left this point late the next afternoon, with well filled canteens; and the uncertainty of finding water in advance, added to this feeling.

We arrived at Leiteresdorffer's Wells soon after sunset, but no water was to be found. The march was continued during the night, and all of the next day, until we arrived at Soldier's Farewell, and no water. The command was strung out a distance of at least five miles; we had been marching thirty hours, with only a canteen each of water, with the thermometer at least 130. A large number of the men had given out and were scattered in parties of three or four, for a dozen miles in the rear.

What was left of the command moved on, and after leaving the wagon road, we arrived in Burro Canon, sometime after dark, where plenty of water was found, when, after taking in a fill, turned into our blankets, entirely forgetting our hunger in our weariness. Company K marched into Burro Canon with less than ten men out of eighty, and it was long after daylight the next day before the whole command had arrived. A short march of twelve miles brought us to Ojo de Baca; thence eighteen miles to the Miembres river.

Our next march, twenty-five miles, was to Cooke's Springs, passing through Cooke's Canon. This location was known by Mexicans as *La Valle del Muerto*, or Valley of Death. It seemed to be rightly named, too, as for nearly two miles were to be seen, on either side, skulls and other portions of human remains who had fallen by Indian assassination. Mounds and crosses were met every few minutes.

As we emerged from this *triste* locality, we encountered the remains of wagons and government stores, that had been destroyed the year before by the regular troops, who had deserted Forts Buchanan and Breckenridge, in Arizona. When they had arrived at this point, they were informed of the surrender of the regulars at Fort Fillmore; consequently, without further inquiry, they destroyed all the government property they had in charge, and made their way, on the west side of the Rio Grande, to Fort Craig.

The next march brought us near to Mule Springs, fifteen miles; and on the next afternoon could be discovered, in the distance, the green, winding way of the Rio Grande, with the Sierras de Organos in the background. Camp was made that night on the banks of the Rio Bravo del Norte, near to old Fort Thorn. The next march was down the west bank of the river to the fording place, known as San Diego, which you will find set down on all maps as a town or village, but to my certain knowledge, up to the time mentioned, and for several years afterwards, there was but one house in the vicinity, and that contained but one room and no roof.

As the river was now, the third of August, at its extreme height, caused by the melting of the snow in the upper Rocky Mountains, we experienced some difficulty in getting our wagons and stores across; still all was completed before sundown, and the next day we arrived at Roblado, near the town of Dona Ana. On the fifth of August, after passing through the villages of Dona Ana and Las Cruces, we arrived at the pleasant town of La Mesilla.

Here was to be our resting place. We found a well-built village, with a numerous population, mostly Mexican. The rebels, who had arrived in the Territory, we learned, had, after the treacherous surrender of the regular troops at Fort Fillmore (directly opposite La Mesilla), marched north. They found Fort Craig too strong to be attacked, and, contrary to all military maxims, had continued on, leaving a fortified position in their rear.

The desperate battle of Val Verde had taken place on the twenty-first and twenty-second of February, 1862, a short distance above Fort Craig. And as long as Major Benny Roberts had command of the Federal troops they were successful, but when General E. R. S. Canby came on the field and took command, the rebels soon had turned the tide of the battle in their favour. McRae's battery was taken, and our troops were returning, panic-stricken, across the river, and fleeing towards Fort Craig, about three miles down the river.

The rebels then approached Albuquerque, where was stored a large amount of government stores, which were surrendered without a struggle. Thence they proceeded to Santa Fe, where, without opposition, they took possession. There was one other fort to be taken, about one hundred miles northwest—Fort Union.

After some delay at Santa Fe, the rebels, numbering some sixteen hundred, set out for Fort Union. At Apache Pass, or Pigeon's Ranch, they were met by a Colorado regiment, with what regulars and militia could be found, all under command of Colonel John P. Slough (afterwards chief justice of the Territory), and were defeated, their wagons, ammunition, and all their stores having been destroyed by a party of Union troops under Captain W. H. Lewis, Fifth United States Infantry, and Captain A. B. Cary, of the Third United States Infantry, who scaled a mountain and got into their rear.

The rebels precipitately retreated from this point, to and down the Rio Grande, having passed La Mesilla a few weeks before our arrival, and left the Territory with about twelve hundred men out of thirty-seven hundred, that they had arrived with.

The different companies of the "Column," as they arrived, were now sent to different points in the department. Our Colonel, James H. Carleton, had been promoted to Brigadier General, and had relieved General E. R. S. Canby, in command of the department of New Mexico. The regular troops were all relieved, except the Fifth Infantry, and sent east, and a protection was now assured to the population, by the California Volunteers. Lieutenant Colonel J. R. West was now promoted to colonel of the regiment, and in command of the southern district of the department.

Fine quarters were found for the command in the village of La Mesilla, and the district was under martial law. Duty was really pleasant here,—plenty of society, with frequent *bailes*, few drills, and plenty of everything to eat and drink. The white population were nearly all of secession proclivities, one in particular, Samuel L. Jones (better known as the pro-slavery Sheriff Jones, of Kansas), who resided here, was arrested usually about once a week, and incarcerated in the guardhouse for treasonable utterances.

After a protracted season of this duty, or up to about the twentieth of November, came the most unpleasant part of the history of Company K. There had been several escapes from the guard-house of persons who had been imprisoned for treasonable utterances, until it seemed that there might exist a disposition among some of the command to be a party to these frequent escapades. This state of affairs existed until one morning an escape was reported to the commanding officer, Colonel West, who immediately ordered the sergeant of the guard, with sentinels numbers one, two, three, four and five, who were on duty at the time, to be placed in the guard-house, in irons.

It so happened that this sergeant and all the sentinels belonged to Company K, and at the morning drill, after guard mount, the company refused to do further duty, or until the irons were taken off of Sergeant Miller. The soldier most aggrieved appeared to be Corporal Charles Smith, or rather he acted as spokesman for the company. The company was immediately ordered into their quarters by Lieutenant Pettis, and put under guard, and the facts reported to the commanding officer.

Orders were given for all prisoners to be placed in the guard-house; Company K was ordered to proceed to the *plaza* or parade without arms, when the long roll was beat. The other two companies of the garrison were soon on the *plaza*, fully equipped. Colonel West now made his appearance, mounted; he then marched Company A, Fifth California Infantry, about five paces in front of and facing Company K, with pieces loaded, and at a "ready." He then called Corporal Smith to the front, and asked him if he still persisted in refusing to do his duty? The Corporal respectfully, but firmly, announced that he would do no duty until the irons were removed from Sergeant Miller.

Company D, First California Infantry, had been wheeled to the right out of line, and the corporal was now ordered to place himself about six paces in front of this company. Upon his again refusing to do duty, Captain Mitchell, of Company D, was ordered to fire upon him. This order was unhesitatingly obeyed; and after the smoke had cleared away, it was seen that the corporal was uninjured.

Not so with some others. The position of Company D was such that it was facing the cathedral, which is situated on the west side of the *plaza*; on either side of the cathedral were long straight streets, running from the *plaza*; the long roll and the other preparations had called all the inhabitants from their residences, and the result of the first volley was to wound two invalid soldiers, together with one Mexican woman and one child, and the cathedral, which was built of *adobes*, was concealed for a few minutes by its own dust, caused by the minie balls penetrating its front.

The corporal was again questioned by Colonel West, who returned his former answer, and Company D again fired a volley, but the corporal remained untouched. After another questioning by the Colonel, Company D was once more ordered to fire, when, between the commands "aim," "fire," Colonel West rode up behind the company with uplifted sabre, and gave the command to "lower those rifles," when the command was given by the Captain to "fire."

At this discharge, the corporal fell to the ground, a minie ball having passed directly through him, having entered his right breast. He was immediately placed upon a stretcher, and expired on his way to the hospital. The rest of the company was now questioned by Colonel West, and each man asserted his willingness to do his duty, when the command was dismissed to their quarters, and Company K immediately assumed their arms and accoutrements and appeared upon the *plaza* for drill. This was the only evidence of insubordination ever shown in the "Column," and the prompt manner in which this one was met and punished, precluded any danger of another exhibition of this character.

A few days after these occurrences, some of our spies and scouts brought in the intelligence that another large party of rebels had left San Antonio, Texas, for New Mexico. Accordingly, Companies K and D were ordered to San Elizario, Texas, a town about twenty-five miles below El Paso, Mexico, and the last point of civilization towards San Antonio, on outpost duty. After remaining here about six weeks, and no rebels appearing, Company K was ordered to Fort Craig. A march of twenty-five miles brought us to Franklin or Fort Bliss, directly opposite El Paso; thence two marches, aggregating fifty miles, found us in our old quarters at La Mesilla, where the company was ordered to remain until the adjournment of a general court-martial which was then in session at that post.

A week later, and Company K commenced its march for Fort Craig. A short march brought us again to Dona Ana. Three miles from that village brought us to the commencement of the much dreaded *Jornada del Muerto* (Journey of Death). The *Jornada* is a large desert, well supplied with fine *gramma* grass in some portions, but absolutely destitute of water or shade for seventy-five miles. Why it ever received its title, I never distinctly learned, but suppose it was on account of the very numerous massacres committed on it by the Apache Indians.

On the east, in the far distance, are the Sierras Blancos, and is fringed on the west by the Sierra Caballo and Sierra de Frey Cristobal. From these heights, on either side, the Indians are enabled to distinctly perceive any party of travellers coming over the wide and unsheltered expanse of the *Jornada del Muerto*. When any such parties are seen, they come sweeping down upon the unsuspecting immigrant in more than usual numbers, and if successful, as they generally are, in their attack, invariably destroy all of the party, for there is no possible chance of escape; and the Apaches never take any prisoners but women and young children, and they become captives for life.

The first camp was a dry one, and as the command was accompanied by a tank of water, drawn by six mules, thus being prepared by a plentiful supply of water, I concluded to cross this desert at my leisure. The next forenoon we passed by the celebrated "Point of Rocks," the company being deployed as skirmishers, with the hope of finding Indians hiding between the huge boulders of which it was composed, but without results. Late in the afternoon we arrived at the Aleman, so called from the fact that a whole German immigrant family had been massacred at this point some years before by the Indians.

The next night another dry camp, having passed during the day the *Laguna del Muerto*, where water is found in some seasons. While some three miles on our left was the *Ojo del Muerto*, a point where Fort McRae was established in 1863 by Captain Henry A. Greene, commanding Company G, First California Infantry, now a resident of this city, (Providence, R. I.). The next day's march brought us to the little village of El Paraje del Fra Cristobal. Near the spot on which the camp was made, was the peaceful flowing and muddy Rio Grande. A short march of five miles brought us to our destination—Fort Craig. Our arrival was in January, 1863.

The company remained at this post during the year 1863, monotony of garrison life being relieved by furnishing escorts to wagon trains bound north and south, and an occasional scout after Indians. In July of that year, Assistant Surgeon Watson, who had been commissioned at Sacramento, California, more than a year before, and had been ordered to report to the headquarters of his regiment at Fort Craig, arrived at Fort McRae, without accident. On leaving that post, Captain Greene had furnished him with one government wagon and an escort of five or six men of his company.

They set out with joyful anticipation; the doctor was delighted to know that after a year's travel, he would soon be at his new home, and be doing duty with his own regiment, which he had never seen. The wagon, with its occupants, soon emerged from the canon of the *Ojo del Muerto*, and came out on the hard, smooth, natural road of the *Jornada*.

About the middle of the afternoon, they were proceeding leisurely along; twelve miles in advance could be plainly seen the buildings of Fort Craig, with "Old Glory" on the flag-staff. The driver of the team, Johnson, a soldier of Greene's company, sat on his near wheel-mule chatting pleasantly with the doctor, who occupied the front of the wagon, with his feet hanging down on the whiffle-trees; the escort were all in the wagon, lying on their blankets, with their arms and equipments beneath them. Within five miles of them there was not a rock, tree, shrub, or bush, as large as a man's head—they felt a perfect security.

Another moment, how changed! There arose from the sand of the desert, where they had buried themselves, some ten or twelve Apaches, within twenty feet of the moving wagon, and poured a volley of arrows into the doomed party, and closing in immediately, a part attacked the occupants of the wagon, while the rest disengaged the mules, and mounting their backs started for the mountains on the west, towards the river, and before the soldiers were out of the wagon were out of reach of their fire.

Doctor Watson was shot with two arrows, one in his right arm, and the other on the inside of his right thigh, severing the femoral artery. He breathed his last in a few minutes; the driver was shot through the heart, and one or two of the escorts were slightly wounded. News of this affair reached the post before sunset, and in twenty minutes Company K was on its way down the west side of the river to intercept, if possible, these murderers. The company was kept in the field for thirty days, without other result than to find a hot trail of eighty-two Navajoes, who were on their way to their own country, with some eight thousand head of sheep and other stock that they had stolen in the upper counties of New Mexico.

As the company were dismounted, it was impossible to take up the trail. The commander of the company, however, with five cavalrymen and two Mexican scouts, followed and overtook the Indians after a run of twenty-five miles, but accomplished nothing except exchanging some twenty or twenty-five shots on either side, as our animals were completely "blown," and eighty-two to eight was an unpleasant disparity of numbers. The lieutenant and his men arrived back at the river the next morning, having been in the saddle nearly twenty-four hours. The result of the short skirmish was that one of the cavalrymen's horses was shot through the breast, and one Navajo was sent to his happy hunting-grounds and one was wounded.

January, 1864, Company K was ordered to Los Pinos, about one hundred miles further up the Rio Grande, and about twenty miles south of Albuquerque; marching through the towns of Socorro, La Limitar, across the sand hills at the foot of the *Sierra de los Ladrones*, or Thieves Mountains; crossing the Rio Puerco, near its affluence with the Rio Grande; thence to Sabinal, La Belen, and Los Lunes.

They remained here until the first of February, when Colonel Kit Carson arrived there from the Navajo country, with some two hundred and fifty-three Navajo Indians, whom he had taken prisoners in his operations against that nation. Orders were received from department headquarters for Company K to proceed with these Indians to the Bosque Redondo, some two hundred and fifty miles down on the Pecos River.

Accordingly, after formally receiving these prisoners and receipting therefore, the command moved out, and on the second night arrived at Carnwell Canon; thence to San Antonio, San Antoinette, Los Placeres and Gallisteo. Thus far the command had moved across the country, but on the day of leaving Gallisteo, the company struck the military road leading from Fort Union to Santa Fe, near the old Peces ruins. The command moved along this road to the village of Tecolote; from here they proceeded down the Pecos River, and arrived at Fort Sumner after eighteen days' marching.

Fort Sumner was a new post, established for the purpose of a reservation for Indians, both Navajo and Apache, that should be taken prisoners by the troops, and Colonel Carson was on a campaign against the Navajoes, in which he was successful, as there were finally some eight thousand of these Indians captured and placed on this reservation. Those brought in by Company K were the first large body that had arrived. I will say here, in parenthesis, that this is the only way to treat the Indian question; for this Indian nation (the Navajoes), after receiving a severe drubbing by Carson, and all had surrendered, were finally allowed to return to their own country, since which time they have continued on the best of terms with our people. This has always been the experience on the frontiers—one effective campaign is better than all the treaties that were ever consummated.

Fort Sumner was at this time in command of Major Henry D. Wallen, United States Seventh Infantry, than whom there was no more excellent gentleman in the service of the government. His administration was marked by a sincere desire to do justice to all under him, a feature that was sadly deficient in too many officers of the time that is spoken of. He was a perfect example of sobriety, and his case certainly was a commendation of the excellence of education of the academy at West Point, of which he was an honoured graduate.

Company K had been at Fort Sumner but a few days when it was ordered to report to the commanding officer at Fort Union, necessitating a march of one hundred and twenty-five miles. The command arrived at Fort Union on the eighteenth day of March, 1864, and remained there, doing camp duty, during the months of April, May and June. In July, the company proceeded, with a company of New Mexican cavalry, towards the east, by the route known as the Cummarron route, passing on our way, Burgwin's Spring, named after the gallant Captain Burgwin, First Regiment United States Dragoons, who fell while leading the attack upon the insurgents at Taos, 1847, and the Wagon Mound, a high landmark (so called from its shape).

From this point to the "Point of Rocks," forty miles, is the track of a bloody, brave and disastrous fight made by eight passengers in the stage against a band of sixty Apaches. They fought every inch of the long, dread struggle. Killed one by one, and dropped on the road, two survivors maintained their defence a long time, and when the sole contestant was left, his last dying effort was to strew the contents of his powder-horn in the sand, and stir it in with his foot, so that the Indians could not use it. Wilson's Creek, some miles further on, is named after a Mr. Wilson, a merchant of Santa Fe, who was overtaken here by the Indians, and, with his wife and child—for he was alone with them—butchered with the usual savage outrage and cruelty.

The command returned to Fort Union in September, in which month the First Infantry, California Volunteers, was mustered out of service, their term of three years having expired, with the exception of Company K, it being recollected that they were enlisted at San Francisco some time after the other companies had been formed. However, the members of that company began, in October, to be dropped out, and when orders arrived at Fort Union for the formation of the Commanche expedition, under Colonel Kit Carson, there remained of the First Infantry Regiment, California Volunteers, one officer (Lieutenant Pettis) and twenty-six enlisted men of Company K. This company accompanied Carson's expedition with two mountain howitzers, mounted on prairie carriages, and rendezvoued at Fort Bascom, on the Canadian river, near the line of Texas.

This expedition consisted as follows: Colonel Christopher Carson, First New Mexico Cavalry, commanding; Colonel Francisco P. Abreu, First New Mexico Infantry; Major William McCleave, First California Cavalry; Captain Emil Fritz, Company B, First California Cavalry, one officer and forty enlisted men; Lieutenant Sullivan Heath, Company K, First California Cavalry, one officer and forty men; Captain Meriam, Company M, First California Cavalry, one officer and thirty-four men; Lieutenant George H. Pettis, Company K, First California Infantry, one officer and twenty-six men; Captain Charles Deus, Company M, First New Mexico Cavalry, two officers and seventy men; Captain Joseph Berney, Company D, First New Mexico Cavalry, two officers and thirty-six men; Company A, First California Veteran Infantry, seventy-five men; Assistant Surgeon George S. Courtright, United States Volunteers, and an officer whose name escapes me, as Assistant Quartermaster and Commissary,—numbering in all, fourteen officers and three hundred and twenty-one enlisted men.

In addition to the command, Colonel Carson had induced seventy-two friendly Indians (Utes and Apaches), and as big scoundrels as there were on the frontiers, by promising them all the plunder that they might acquire, to join the expedition.

On the sixth of November, the command left Fort Bascom, and proceeded down on the north bank of the Canadian, hoping to find the Commanche and Kiowa Indians (who had been committing their atrocities during the whole of 1864) in their winter quarters. The Indians with our command, on every night, after making camp, being now on the war-path, indulged in the accustomed war dance, which, although new to most of us, became almost intolerable, it being kept up each night until nearly day-break; and until we became accustomed to their groans and howlings, incident to the dance, it was impossible to sleep. Each morning of our march, two of our Indians would be sent ahead several hours before we started, who would return to camp at night and report.

We had been on our march day after day without particular incident until our arrival at Mule Creek, when our scouts brought in the intelligence that they had seen signs of a large body of Indians that had moved that day, and that they could be overtaken without much effort. Immediately after supper, all of the Cavalry, with Company K, moved out of camp in light marching order, leaving the infantry, under command of Colonel Abreu, to protect the wagon train and proceed on our trail on the morrow.

Colonel Carson and command marched all night, except a short halt just before dawn, and struck an outpost of the enemy on the opposite side of the river, at about sunrise, who being mounted retreated, followed by our Indians and two companies of our Cavalry. The rest of the command moved down on the north side of the river, and a few miles below the cavalry struck a Kiowa *rancheria* of one hundred and seventy-six lodges, the Indians retreating down the river on their approach.

Company K, escorted by Lieutenant Heath's command, and accompanied by Colonel Carson, could not advance with the rapidity of the cavalry, as the cannoneers were dismounted, and the wheels tracking very narrow, caused the utmost attention to prevent their being overturned. The Indians from the Kiowa encampment retreated until they were reinforced by a large force of Commanches from a Commanche *rancheria* of five hundred lodges, a short distance below the "Adobe Walls," a location well known by all frontiersmen. The cavalry made a stand here, and were engaged in skirmishing with the enemy, when Company K came on the field with the two mountain howitzers.

An order from Colonel Carson to Lieutenant Pettis to "fling a few shell over thar!" indicating with his hand a large body of Indians who appeared to be about to charge into our forces, that officer immediately ordered "Battery halt! action right, load with shell—load!" Before the fourth discharge of the howitzers, the Indians had retreated out of range, and it was supposed that there would be no more fighting; but we counted without our host, for our animals had scarcely been watered when the enemy returned to the conflict. The horses of the cavalry were again placed in the "Adobe Walls," which were elevated enough to protect them from the rifle balls of the enemy, and the fight was soon at its height.

About the middle of the afternoon, Carson concluded to return to the Kiowa village that we had passed through in the morning, contrary to the wishes of his officers, who were anxious to advance to the Commanche village, which was less than a mile in our front. The return column consisted of the cavalry horses, the number four of each set of fours leading the other three horses, with the howitzers in the rear, the dismounted cavalry acting as skirmishers on the front, rear and either flank. The firing was continued from each side until the village was reached, when our troops proceeded to destroy it, which was effectually done before dark.

A further march of about four miles, and the wagon train was reached, the safety of which had been the subject of much anxiety during the day. The gun carriages and ammunition carts of Company K were packed with the wounded on their return from the Kiowa village. A rest was had the next day, which was sadly needed, as the whole command had been marching and fighting about twenty-seven hours, on a few broken hard tack and a slice of salt pork each. The second day after the fight, Carson concluded to return to Fort Bascom, which post was reached in twenty-one days.

Here the command remained until orders were received from General Carleton, commanding the department, and Company K was ordered to Fort Union, as the term of service of nearly all the men had expired. By the first of February, 1865, all the enlisted men of the company had been mustered out of service, and Lieutenant Pettis, the last man of his regiment, was ordered to report to the mustering officer at Santa Fe, with all the records of his company; and on the fifteenth of February, he was mustered out of service, and Company K, First Infantry, California Volunteers, had ceased to exist, having marched on foot during its term of service four thousand two hundred and forty-five miles.

LEONAUR

ALSO FROM LEONAUR
AVAILABLE IN SOFTCOVER OR HARDCOVER WITH DUST JACKET

JOURNALS OF ROBERT ROGERS OF THE RANGERS by Robert Rogers—The exploits of Rogers & the Rangers in his own words during 1755-1761 in the French & Indian War.

GALLOPING GUNS by James Young—The Experiences of an Officer of the Bengal Horse Artillery During the Second Maratha War 1804-1805.

GORDON by Demetrius Charles Boulger—The Career of Gordon of Khartoum.

THE BATTLE OF NEW ORLEANS by Zachary F. Smith—The final major engagement of the War of 1812.

THE TWO WARS OF MRS DUBERLY by Frances Isabella Duberly—An Intrepid Victorian Lady's Experience of the Crimea and Indian Mutiny.

WITH THE GUARDS' BRIGADE DURING THE BOER WAR by Edward P. Lowry—On Campaign from Bloemfontein to Koomati Poort and Back.

THE REBELLIOUS DUCHESS by Paul F. S. Dermoncourt—The Adventures of the Duchess of Berri and Her Attempt to Overthrow French Monarchy.

MEN OF THE MUTINY by John Tulloch Nash & Henry Metcalfe—Two Accounts of the Great Indian Mutiny of 1857: Fighting with the Bengal Yeomanry Cavalry & Private Metcalfe at Lucknow.

CAMPAIGN IN THE CRIMEA by George Shuldham Peard—The Recollections of an Officer of the 20th Regiment of Foot.

WITHIN SEBASTOPOL by K. Hodasevich—A Narrative of the Campaign in the Crimea, and of the Events of the Siege.

WITH THE CAVALRY TO AFGHANISTAN by William Taylor—The Experiences of a Trooper of H. M. 4th Light Dragoons During the First Afghan War.

THE CAWNPORE MAN by Mowbray Thompson—A First Hand Account of the Siege and Massacre During the Indian Mutiny By One of Four Survivors.

BRIGADE COMMANDER: AFGHANISTAN by Henry Brooke—The Journal of the Commander of the 2nd Infantry Brigade, Kandahar Field Force During the Second Afghan War.

BANCROFT OF THE BENGAL HORSE ARTILLERY by N. W. Bancroft—An Account of the First Sikh War 1845-1846.

LEONAUR

ALSO FROM LEONAUR

AVAILABLE IN SOFTCOVER OR HARDCOVER WITH DUST JACKET

ADVENTURES OF A YOUNG RIFLEMAN *by Johann Christian Maempel*—The Experiences of a Saxon in the French & British Armies During the Napoleonic Wars.

THE HUSSAR *by Norbert Landsheit & G. R. Gleig*—A German Cavalryman in British Service Throughout the Napoleonic Wars.

RECOLLECTIONS OF THE PENINSULA *by Moyle Sherer*—An Officer of the 34th Regiment of Foot—'The Cumberland Gentlemen'—on Campaign Against Napoleon's French Army in Spain.

MARINE OF REVOLUTION & CONSULATE *by Moreau de Jonnès*—The Recollections of a French Soldier of the Revolutionary Wars 1791-1804.

GENTLEMEN IN RED *by John Dobbs & Robert Knowles*—Two Accounts of British Infantry Officers During the Peninsular War Recollections of an Old 52nd Man by John Dobbs An Officer of Fusiliers by Robert Knowles.

CORPORAL BROWN'S CAMPAIGNS IN THE LOW COUNTRIES *by Robert Brown*—Recollections of a Coldstream Guard in the Early Campaigns Against Revolutionary France 1793-1795.

THE 7TH (QUEENS OWN) HUSSARS: Volume 2—1793-1815 *by C. R. B. Barrett*—During the Campaigns in the Low Countries & the Peninsula and Waterloo Campaigns of the Napoleonic Wars. Volume 2: 1793-1815.

THE MARENGO CAMPAIGN 1800 *by Herbert H. Sargent*—The Victory that Completed the Austrian Defeat in Italy.

DONALDSON OF THE 94TH—SCOTS BRIGADE *by Joseph Donaldson*—The Recollections of a Soldier During the Peninsula & South of France Campaigns of the Napoleonic Wars.

A CONSCRIPT FOR EMPIRE *by Philippe as told to Johann Christian Maempel*—The Experiences of a Young German Conscript During the Napoleonic Wars.

JOURNAL OF THE CAMPAIGN OF 1815 *by Alexander Cavalié Mercer*—The Experiences of an Officer of the Royal Horse Artillery During the Waterloo Campaign.

NAPOLEON'S CAMPAIGNS IN POLAND 1806-7 *by Robert Wilson*—The campaign in Poland from the Russian side of the conflict.

LEONAUR

ALSO FROM LEONAUR
AVAILABLE IN SOFTCOVER OR HARDCOVER WITH DUST JACKET

COLBORNE: A SINGULAR TALENT FOR WAR *by John Colborne*—The Napoleonic Wars Career of One of Wellington's Most Highly Valued Officers in Egypt, Holland, Italy, the Peninsula and at Waterloo.

NAPOLEON'S RUSSIAN CAMPAIGN *by Philippe Henri de Segur*—The Invasion, Battles and Retreat by an Aide-de-Camp on the Emperor's Staff.

WITH THE LIGHT DIVISION *by John H. Cooke*—The Experiences of an Officer of the 43rd Light Infantry in the Peninsula and South of France During the Napoleonic Wars.

WELLINGTON AND THE PYRENEES CAMPAIGN VOLUME I: FROM VITORIA TO THE BIDASSOA *by F. C. Beatson*—The final phase of the campaign in the Iberian Peninsula.

WELLINGTON AND THE INVASION OF FRANCE VOLUME II: THE BIDASSOA TO THE BATTLE OF THE NIVELLE *by F. C. Beatson*—The final phase of the campaign in the Iberian Peninsula.

WELLINGTON AND THE FALL OF FRANCE VOLUME III: THE GAVES AND THE BATTLE OF ORTHEZ *by F. C. Beatson*—The final phase of the campaign in the Iberian Peninsula.

NAPOLEON'S IMPERIAL GUARD: FROM MARENGO TO WATERLOO *by J. T. Headley*—The story of Napoleon's Imperial Guard and the men who commanded them.

BATTLES & SIEGES OF THE PENINSULAR WAR *by W. H. Fitchett*—Corunna, Busaco, Albuera, Ciudad Rodrigo, Badajos, Salamanca, San Sebastian & Others.

SERGEANT GUILLEMARD: THE MAN WHO SHOT NELSON? *by Robert Guillemard*—A Soldier of the Infantry of the French Army of Napoleon on Campaign Throughout Europe.

WITH THE GUARDS ACROSS THE PYRENEES *by Robert Batty*—The Experiences of a British Officer of Wellington's Army During the Battles for the Fall of Napoleonic France, 1813 .

A STAFF OFFICER IN THE PENINSULA *by E. W. Buckham*—An Officer of the British Staff Corps Cavalry During the Peninsula Campaign of the Napoleonic Wars.

THE LEIPZIG CAMPAIGN: 1813—NAPOLEON AND THE "BATTLE OF THE NATIONS" *by F. N. Maude*—Colonel Maude's analysis of Napoleon's campaign of 1813 around Leipzig.

LEONAUR

ALSO FROM LEONAUR
AVAILABLE IN SOFTCOVER OR HARDCOVER WITH DUST JACKET

BUGEAUD: A PACK WITH A BATON *by Thomas Robert Bugeaud*—The Early Campaigns of a Soldier of Napoleon's Army Who Would Become a Marshal of France.

WATERLOO RECOLLECTIONS *by Frederick Llewellyn*—Rare First Hand Accounts, Letters, Reports and Retellings from the Campaign of 1815.

SERGEANT NICOL *by Daniel Nicol*—The Experiences of a Gordon Highlander During the Napoleonic Wars in Egypt, the Peninsula and France.

THE JENA CAMPAIGN: 1806 *by F. N. Maude*—The Twin Battles of Jena & Auerstadt Between Napoleon's French and the Prussian Army.

PRIVATE O'NEIL *by Charles O'Neil*—The recollections of an Irish Rogue of H. M. 28th Regt.—The Slashers—during the Peninsula & Waterloo campaigns of the Napoleonic war.

ROYAL HIGHLANDER *by James Anton*—A soldier of H.M 42nd (Royal) Highlanders during the Peninsular, South of France & Waterloo Campaigns of the Napoleonic Wars.

CAPTAIN BLAZE *by Elzéar Blaze*—Life in Napoleons Army.

LEJEUNE VOLUME 1 *by Louis-François Lejeune*—The Napoleonic Wars through the Experiences of an Officer on Berthier's Staff.

LEJEUNE VOLUME 2 *by Louis-François Lejeune*—The Napoleonic Wars through the Experiences of an Officer on Berthier's Staff.

CAPTAIN COIGNET *by Jean-Roch Coignet*—A Soldier of Napoleon's Imperial Guard from the Italian Campaign to Russia and Waterloo.

FUSILIER COOPER *by John S. Cooper*—Experiences in the 7th (Royal) Fusiliers During the Peninsular Campaign of the Napoleonic Wars and the American Campaign to New Orleans.

FIGHTING NAPOLEON'S EMPIRE *by Joseph Anderson*—The Campaigns of a British Infantryman in Italy, Egypt, the Peninsular & the West Indies During the Napoleonic Wars.

CHASSEUR BARRES *by Jean-Baptiste Barres*—The experiences of a French Infantryman of the Imperial Guard at Austerlitz, Jena, Eylau, Friedland, in the Peninsular, Lutzen, Bautzen, Zinnwald and Hanau during the Napoleonic Wars.

![LEONAUR logo]

ALSO FROM LEONAUR
AVAILABLE IN SOFTCOVER OR HARDCOVER WITH DUST JACKET

CAPTAIN COIGNET *by Jean-Roch Coignet*—A Soldier of Napoleon's Imperial Guard from the Italian Campaign to Russia and Waterloo.

HUSSAR ROCCA *by Albert Jean Michel de Rocca*—A French cavalry officer's experiences of the Napoleonic Wars and his views on the Peninsular Campaigns against the Spanish, British And Guerilla Armies.

MARINES TO 95TH (RIFLES) *by Thomas Fernyhough*—The military experiences of Robert Fernyhough during the Napoleonic Wars.

LIGHT BOB *by Robert Blakeney*—The experiences of a young officer in H.M 28th & 36th regiments of the British Infantry during the Peninsular Campaign of the Napoleonic Wars 1804 - 1814.

WITH WELLINGTON'S LIGHT CAVALRY *by William Tomkinson*—The Experiences of an officer of the 16th Light Dragoons in the Peninsular and Waterloo campaigns of the Napoleonic Wars.

SERGEANT BOURGOGNE *by Adrien Bourgogne*—With Napoleon's Imperial Guard in the Russian Campaign and on the Retreat from Moscow 1812 - 13.

SURTEES OF THE 95TH (RIFLES) *by William Surtees*—A Soldier of the 95th (Rifles) in the Peninsular campaign of the Napoleonic Wars.

SWORDS OF HONOUR *by Henry Newbolt & Stanley L. Wood*—The Careers of Six Outstanding Officers from the Napoleonic Wars, the Wars for India and the American Civil War.

ENSIGN BELL IN THE PENINSULAR WAR *by George Bell*—The Experiences of a young British Soldier of the 34th Regiment 'The Cumberland Gentlemen' in the Napoleonic wars.

HUSSAR IN WINTER *by Alexander Gordon*—A British Cavalry Officer during the retreat to Corunna in the Peninsular campaign of the Napoleonic Wars.

THE COMPLEAT RIFLEMAN HARRIS *by Benjamin Harris as told to and transcribed by Captain Henry Curling, 52nd Regt. of Foot*—The adventures of a soldier of the 95th (Rifles) during the Peninsular Campaign of the Napoleonic Wars.

THE ADVENTURES OF A LIGHT DRAGOON *by George Farmer & G.R. Gleig*—A cavalryman during the Peninsular & Waterloo Campaigns, in captivity & at the siege of Bhurtpore, India.

www.ingramcontent.com/pod-product-compliance
Lightning Source LLC
Chambersburg PA
CBHW031857090426
42741CB00005B/527